THE SEMINAR OF
JACQUES LACAN

BOOK XX

By Jacques Lacan

THE SEMINAR OF JACQUES LACAN

Edited by Jacques-Alain Miller

On Feminine Sexuality
The Limits of Love and Knowledge

BOOK XX

Encore 1972–1973

TRANSLATED WITH NOTES BY

Bruce Fink

W · W · NORTON & COMPANY

NEW YORK   LONDON

Originally published in French as LE SEMINAIRE, LIVRE XX, ENCORE,
1972–1973 by Editions du Seuil, Paris, 1975

Norton gratefully acknowledges financial assistance provided by the
French Ministry of Culture for the translation of this book.

Library of Congress Cataloging in Publication Data

Lacan, Jacques, 1901–
[Encore 1972–1972. English]
On feminine sexuality : the limits of love and knowledge / Jacques
Lacan ; translated with notes by Bruce Fink.
p.   cm. — (The Seminar of Jacques Lacan ; bk. 20)
Includes bibliographical references and index.
ISBN 0-393-04573-0
1. Sex (Psychology) 2. Psychoanalysis. 3. Lacan, Jacques, 1901–
Jacques Lacan. English ; bk. 20.
BF175.5.S48L3313 1998
150.19'5—dc21   9743225
                                                              CIP

ISBN 0-393-31916-4 pbk.
ISBN 13 978-0-393-31916-3 pbk.

W. W. Norton & Company, Inc.
500 Fifth Avenue, New York, N.Y. 10110
www.wwnorton.com

W. W. Norton & Company Ltd.
15 Carlisle Street, London W1D 3BS

0

CONTENTS

PREFACE

This translation is long overdue. Published in French in 1975, this groundbreaking Seminar – including some of Lacan's most sophisticated work on love, desire, and jouissance – could well have appeared in English around the same time as the early *Écrits: A Selection* (1977) and *The Four Fundamental Concepts of Psychoanalysis* (Seminar XI, 1978). In its absence, Lacan, instead of *presenting himself* to the English-speaking world, has been believed by many to be faithfully presented to us by certain of his one-time students – such as Julia Kristeva and Luce Irigaray, though their views diverge substantially from his on many points – and by a spate of American, Australian, and British critics who have, in my view, grossly misrepresented him.

This translation, long-awaited by the public and by me – I always wanted copies to distribute to students and colleagues, though I never expected to be given the opportunity to translate it myself until the day Jacques-Alain Miller and Norton proposed it to me – is thus offered up in the hope of rekindling debate on the basis of something closer to what Lacan actually said, and quieting the kinds of banal reductions of Lacan's views to pat phrases derived from commentaries on commentaries on commentaries that currently pass for serious academic discourse.

I have not deliberately tried to vindicate my own previously published interpretation of Lacan's view of sexual difference in this translation, attempting instead to remain open to being surprised by his formulations (and, indeed, I was surprised!). Nevertheless, Lacan's French is – as anyone who has made a serious attempt to grapple with it is aware – so polyvalent and ambiguous that some frame must be imposed to make any sense of it whatsoever. As is true in the case of an analyst listening to the discourse proffered by an analysand, there is no escaping a theoretical frame of sorts – for without some frame one hears nothing or simply falls back on the ready-made frame provided by pop psychology – and the challenge to the analyst and translator alike is to keep the frame flexible enough to hear what is new, and to keep oneself flexible enough to adjust part or all of the frame accordingly.

The frame I rely on here is, as I hope will be apparent to the reader, the larger context of Lacan's work, including the complete *Écrits* (the 925 pages of which I am currently translating and retranslating for Norton), virtually all of Lacan's seminars, and other of Lacan's writings and lectures as well. I have striven to make sense of what Lacan says here in the context of what he said before and afterward. His work obviously fits into a historical, philosophical, literary, and psychiatric context as well, all the elements of which no one person could ever hope to master. Russell Grigg (the translator of Seminar III, *The Psychoses*, who is currently translating Seminar XVII) and Héloïse Fink were very helpful in providing such references. Readers of this translation are encouraged to write to me care of the publisher regarding specialized vocabulary and specific works and authors alluded to that I may have overlooked. Adequate translation of Lacan's work is a long-term project to which many people in many fields should contribute.

A word here about my translation "strategy": I have sought to keep the translation itself as "clean" and flowing as possible, and this has led me to relegate some complex phraseology and discussion of alternative readings to the footnotes. It seems to me that the impact of certain passages is easily defused by the inclusion of too many slashes, parenthetical remarks, and unusual typography (of which Lacan himself provides enough). I have endeavored throughout to make the English translation have as powerful an effect on the English reader as the French does on the French, and this can only be obtained by occasionally nailing down meanings more tightly than might be hoped for the purposes of extensive commentary. On such occasions I have dropped footnotes detailing what may well have been lopped off.

I am grateful to Russell Grigg who, in his thorough reading of Chapter I of this translation, reminded me once again of just how many alternative readings are possible. Héloïse Fink provided invaluable assistance by checking the *entire* French and English texts line by line and spending countless hours patiently pouring over Lacan's quirky grammar and endless ambiguities with me. I alone am responsible for the inaccuracies that inevitably remain.

Certain readers may need to be reminded that this was not a text at all originally, but rather a series of largely improvised talks given from notes. The French editor of the Seminar, Jacques-Alain Miller, had to work from a stenographer's faulty transcription of those talks, and was obliged to invent spellings for certain of Lacan's neologisms and condensations and new ways of punctuating for Lacan's idiosyncratic speech. All of the paragraph breaks here follow the French text, and much of the punctuation here is modeled on that adopted by Miller and approved of by Lacan.

Few texts in the Lacanian opus are as difficult to render into English as this one, given Lacan's myriad word plays and his ever more polyvalent, evocative style. I can only hope – as I have said elsewhere – that my translation here "compensates" the reader for the inevitable loss in plurivocity with *another satisfaction*.

Bruce Fink

I

On jouissance

It so happened that I did not publish *The Ethics of Psychoanalysis*.[1] At the time, it was a form of politeness on my part – after you, be my guest, be my *worst*. . . .[2] With the passage of time, I learned that I could say a little more about it. And then I realized that what constituted my course was a sort of "I don't want to know anything about it."

That is no doubt why, with the passage of time, I am still *(encore)* here, and you are too. I never cease to be amazed by it. . . .[3]

What has worked in my favor for a while is that there is also on your part, in the great mass of you who are here, an "I don't want to know anything about it." But – the all important question – is it the same one?

Is your "I don't want to know anything about it" regarding a certain knowledge that is transmitted to you bit by bit what is at work in me? I don't think so, and it is precisely because you suppose that I begin from a different place than you in this "I don't want to know anything about it" that you find yourselves attached *(liés)* to me. Such that, while it is true that with respect to you I can only be here in the position of an analysand due to my "I don't want to know anything about it," it'll be quite some time before you reach the same point.

That is why it is only when yours seems adequate to you that you can, if

[1] Lacan's 1959–1960 seminar, entitled *L'éthique de la psychanalyse*, has since been edited by Jacques-Alain Miller, published in French (Paris: Seuil, 1986), and translated into English by Dennis Porter as *The Ethics of Psychoanalysis* (New York: Norton, 1992). (N.B.: All the footnotes provided in this translation of Seminar XX are the translator's notes.)

[2] Lacan is playing here on several terms and registers at once: in *je vous en prie, je vous en pire, prie* ("beg," as in "I beg of you") and *pire* ("worse") are anagrams; *en pire* is pronounced in the same way as *empire* (to worsen or deteriorate); and Lacan's seminar the year before this one (Seminar XIX, 1971–1972, unpublished) was entitled . . . *ou pire (. . . or Worse)*.

[3] Lacan manages to work the term *encore* into this sentence as well. Less idiomatically put, it could be translated: "I am still *(encore)* always astonished by it. . . ."

you are one of my analysands, normally detach yourself from your analysis. The conclusion I draw from this is that, contrary to what people have been saying, there is no contradiction between my position as an analyst and what I do here.

1

Last year I entitled what I thought I could say to you, . . . *ou pire (. . . or Worse)*, and then, *Ça s'oupire*.[4] That has nothing to do with "I" or "you" – *je ne t'oupire pas, ni tu ne m'oupires.* Our path, that of analytic discourse, progresses only due to this narrow limit, this cutting edge of the knife, which is such that elsewhere it can only get worse *(s'oupirer)*.

That is the discourse that underpins *(supporte)*[5] my work, and to begin it anew this year, I am first of all going to assume that you are in bed, a bed employed to its fullest, there being two of you in it.

To someone, a jurist, who had been kind enough to inquire about my discourse, I felt I could respond – in order to give him a sense of its foundation, namely, that language[6] is not the speaking being – that I did not feel out of place having to speak in a law school, since it is the school in which the existence of codes makes it clear that language consists therein and is separate, having been constituted over the ages, whereas speaking beings, known as men, are something else altogether. Thus, to begin by assuming that you are in bed requires that I apologize to him.

I won't leave this bed today, and I will remind the jurist that law basically talks about what I am going to talk to you about – jouissance.

Law does not ignore the bed. Take, for example, the fine common law on which the practice of concubinage, which means to sleep together, is based. What I am going to do is begin with what remains veiled in law,

---

[4] *Soupirer* means "to sigh," but the apostrophe Lacan adds creates a neologism here, a reflexive: "or-sighs itself," "or-is-sighed," "or-worsens itself." Lacan tells us in the next sentence that this invented verb does not work with "I" or "you," at least in part because the *s* of *soupirer* disappears when conjugated as Lacan conjugates it and the reflexivity drops out: "I do not or-worsen you nor do you or-worsen me."
[5] The verb Lacan uses here, *supporter*, recurs constantly in this seminar (and elsewhere in his work as well) and requires a word of explanation. In ordinary French, it most commonly means to bear, stand, or put up with, and is primarily used negatively (e.g., *Je ne le supporte pas*, "I can't stand him"). Even in the present context in the text, this possible sense cannot be entirely ruled out: while psychoanalytic discourse is "behind" Lacan, supporting, backing, bolstering, underpinning, sustaining, carrying, or corroborating what he says, it could also be understood as "putting up with" Lacan. While *supporter* has often been translated as "to prop up" or "propping," I have generally preferred to employ locutions using the verb "to base" and the noun "basis."
[6] Throughout this seminar, I always translate *langage* as language; when I translate *langue* as language, I always include the French in brackets.

namely, what we do in that bed – squeeze each other tight *(s'étreindre)*. I begin with the limit, a limit with which one must indeed begin if one is to be serious, in other words, to establish the series of that which approaches it.

A word here to shed light on the relationship between law *(droit)* and jouissance. "Usufruct" – that's a legal notion, isn't it? – brings together in one word what I already mentioned in my seminar on ethics, namely, the difference between utility[7] and jouissance. What purpose does utility serve? That has never been well defined owing to the prodigious respect speaking beings have, due to language, for means. "Usufruct" means that you can enjoy *(jouir de)*[8] your means, but must not waste them. When you have the usufruct of an inheritance, you can enjoy the inheritance *(en jouir)* as long as you don't use up too much of it. That is clearly the essence of law – to divide up, distribute, or reattribute everything that counts as jouissance.

What is jouissance? Here it amounts to no more than a negative instance *(instance)*.[9] Jouissance is what serves no purpose *(ne sert à rien)*.

I am pointing here to the reservation implied by the field of the right-to-jouissance. Right *(droit)* is not duty. Nothing forces anyone to enjoy *(jouir)* except the superego. The superego is the imperative of jouissance – Enjoy!

Here we see the turning point investigated by analytic discourse. Along this pathway, during the "after you" period of time I let go by, I tried to show that analysis does not allow us to remain at the level of what I began with, respectfully of course – namely, Aristotle's ethics. A kind of slippage occurred in the course of time that did not constitute progress but rather a skirting of the problem, slipping from Aristotle's view of being to Bentham's utilitarianism, in other words, to the theory of fictions,[10] demonstrating the use value – that is, the instrumental status – of language. It is from that standpoint that I return to question the status of being,[11] from the sovereign good as an object of contemplation, on the basis of which people formerly believed they could edify an ethics.

Thus, I am leaving you to your own devices on this bed. I am going out,

---

[7] Lacan's term here, *l'utile*, literally means "the useful."

[8] It should be kept in mind that *jouir de* means to enjoy, take advantage of, benefit from, get off on, and so on. *Jouir* also means "to come" in the sexual sense: "to reach orgasm."

[9] Lacan's *instance*, like Freud's *Instanz*, is often translated as "agency." However, *instance* also implies a power or authority (as when we speak of a Court of the First Instance), and an *insistent*, urgent force, activity, or intervention; it also conveys a note of instantaneousness. "Agency" in no way conveys the *insistence* so important to Lacan's use of the term.

[10] See *Bentham's Theory of Fictions* (Paterson: Littlefield, Adams & Co., 1959); Lacan discusses Bentham in Seminar VII on pages 12, 187, and 228–229.

[11] The French here, *ce qu'il en est de l'être*, is very imprecise, and could be translated as the nature of being, the status of being, or how being stands. Lacan repeatedly uses the locution *ce qu'il en est de* in this seminar in talking about being.

and once again I will write on the door so that, as you exit, you may perhaps recall the dreams you will have pursued on this bed. I will write the following sentence: "Jouissance of the Other," of the Other with a capital O, "of the body of the Other who symbolizes the Other, is not the sign of love."[12]

2

I write that, but I don't write after it "the end," "amen," or "so be it."

Love, of course, constitutes a sign *(fait signe)*[13] and is always mutual.

I put forward that idea a long time ago, very gently, by saying that feelings are always mutual. I did so in order to be asked, "Then what, then what, of love, of love – is it always mutual?" "But of course, but of course!" That is why the unconscious was invented – so that we would realize that man's desire is the Other's desire, and that love, while it is a passion that involves ignorance of desire,[14] nevertheless leaves desire its whole import. When we look a bit more closely, we see the ravages wreaked by this.

Jouissance – jouissance of the Other's body – remains a question, because the answer it may constitute is not necessary. We can take this further still: it is not a sufficient answer either, because love demands love. It never stops *(ne cesse pas)* demanding it. It demands it . . . *encore*. *"Encore"* is the proper name of the gap *(faille)* in the Other from which the demand for love stems.

Where then does what is able, in a way that is neither necessary nor sufficient, to answer with jouissance of the Other's body stem from?

It's not love. It is what last year, inspired in a sense by the chapel at Sainte-Anne Hospital that got on my nerves, I let myself go so far as to call *l'amur*.[15]

L'amur is what appears in the form of bizarre signs on the body. They are

---

[12] The French here is open to a number of different readings: *La jouissance de l'Autre*[. . .], *du corps de l'Autre qui le symbolise, n'est pas le signe de l'amour*. In the first part of the sentence, *jouissance de l'Autre* can mean either the Other's jouissance or one's jouissance/enjoyment of the Other; in the second part of the sentence, there seems, at first glance, to be a typographical error, as Lacan sometimes talks about the other *(autre)* who symbolizes or incarnates the Other *(Autre)* for someone. An alternative reading would be: "The Other's jouissance," that of the Other with a capital O, "[the jouissance] of the body of the Other who symbolizes the Other, is not the sign of love."

[13] *Fait signe* also means gives a sign, signals (something to someone), and plays the part of a sign.

[14] Ignorance is, according to Lacan (and others, including Plato), the strongest of the three passions: ignorance, love, and hate. On the three passions, see, for example, "Direction of the Treatment," *Écrits*, 627. An alternative reading of *le désir de l'homme, c'est le désir de l'Autre* earlier in the sentence would be "man's desire is for the Other's desire."

[15] A combination of *mur* ("wall") and *amour* ("love"). This term was introduced by Lacan on January 6, 1972. *Amure* (pronounced like Lacan's *amur*) is an old sailor's term for tack.

the sexual characteristics that come from beyond, from that place we believed we could eye under the microscope in the form of the germ cell[16] – regarding which I would point out that we can't say that it's life since it also bears death, the death of the body, by repeating it. That is where the *en-corps* comes from.[17] It is thus false to say that there is a separation of the soma from the germ because, since it harbors this germ, the body bears its traces. There are traces on *l'amur.*

But they are only traces. The body's being *(l'être du corps)* is of course sexed *(sexué)*,[18] but it is secondary, as they say. And as experience shows, the body's jouissance, insofar as that body symbolizes the Other, does not depend on those traces.

That can be gathered from the simplest consideration of things.

Then what is involved in love? Is love – as psychoanalysis claims with an audacity that is all the more incredible as all of its experience runs counter to that very notion, and as it demonstrates the contrary – is love about making one *(faire un)?* Is Eros a tension toward the One?

People have been talking about nothing but the One for a long time. "There's such a thing as One" *(Y a d' l'Un)*.[19] I based my discourse last year on that statement, certainly not in order to contribute to this earliest of confusions, for desire merely leads us to aim at the gap *(faille)* where it can be demonstrated that the One is based only on *(tenir de)* the essence of the signifier. I investigated Frege at the beginning [of last year's seminar][20]

---

[16] The French *germen* ("germ" or "germ cell," i.e., the sexual reproductive cell) is contrasted with *soma*, the body of an organism.

[17] *En-corps* is pronounced like *encore*, but literally means "in-body."

[18] *L'être du corps* could also be translated as the being of the body, being qua body, the body qua being, and so on. *Sexué* means having a sex, a sexual organ, or being *differentiated* into male and female, i.e., sexually differentiated. The English word "sexed," used here to translate *sexué(e)*, has the current disadvantage of being associated with the expressions "over-sexed" and "under-sexed," thereby suggesting something *quantitative* about the sexual drives that is not intended in the French. Note the close relation between *sexué* and *sexuation* (translated in this seminar as "sexuation"). *Sexué* and *asexué* are also translated as "sexual" and "asexual," respectively, in certain contexts (e.g., sexual or asexual reproduction).

In the next sentence, "the body's jouissance" could also be translated as "jouissance of the body."

[19] *Y a d' l'Un* is by no means an immediately comprehensible expression, even to the French ear, but the first sense seems to be "There's such a thing as One" (or "the One") or "There's something like One" (or "the One"); in neither case is the emphasis on the "thing" or on quantity. "The One happens," we might even say. A detailed discussion of Seminar XIX would be required to justify the translation I've provided here, but at least two things should be briefly pointed out: *Y a d' l'Un* must be juxtaposed with *Il n'y a pas de rapport sexuel*, there's no such thing as a sexual relationship (see Seminar XIX, May 17, 1972); and Lacan is *not* saying "there's some One" (in the sense of some quantity of One) since he is talking about the One of "pure difference" (see Seminar XIX, June 1, 1972).

[20] See Seminar XIX, December 8, 1971. Lacan discusses Frege in a number of earlier seminars as well, for example, in Seminar XV, March 13, 1968.

in the attempt to demonstrate the gap *(béance)* there is between this One and something that is related to *(tenir à)* being and, behind being, to jouissance.

I can tell you a little tale, that of a parakeet that was in love with Picasso. How could one tell? From the way the parakeet nibbled the collar of his shirt and the flaps of his jacket. Indeed, the parakeet was in love with what is essential to man, namely, his attire *(accoutrement)*. The parakeet was like Descartes, to whom men were merely clothes *(habits)* . . . walking about *(en . . . pro-ménade)*. Clothes promise debauchery *(ça promet la ménade)*, when one takes them off. But this is only a myth, a myth that converges with the bed I mentioned earlier. To enjoy a body *(jouir d'un corps)* when there are no more clothes leaves intact the question of what makes the One, that is, the question of identification. The parakeet identified with Picasso clothed *(habillé)*.

The same goes for everything involving love. The habit loves the monk,[21] as they are but one thereby. In other words, what lies under the habit, what we call the body, is perhaps but the remainder *(reste)*[22] I call object *a*.

What holds the image together is a remainder. Analysis demonstrates that love, in its essence, is narcissistic, and reveals that the substance of what is supposedly object-like *(objectal)*[23] – what a bunch of bull – is in fact that which constitutes a remainder in desire, namely, its cause, and sustains desire through its lack of satisfaction *(insatisfaction)*, and even its impossibility.

Love is impotent, though mutual, because it is not aware that it is but the desire to be One, which leads us to the impossibility of establishing the relationship between "them-two" *(la relation d'eux)*.[24] The relationship between them-two what? – them-two sexes.

3

Assuredly, what appears on bodies in the enigmatic form of sexual characteristics – which are merely secondary – makes sexed beings *(êtres sexués)*. No doubt.[25] But being is the jouissance of the body as such, that is, as asexual *(asexué)*, because what is known as sexual jouissance is marked

13

---

[21] The French expression, sometimes attributed to Rabelais, *l'habit ne fait pas le moine* (literally, "the habit does not make the monk," figuratively, "don't judge a book by its cover" or "appearances can be deceiving"), is adapted here by Lacan: *l'habit aime le moine*, "the habit loves the monk."

[22] *Reste* can take on many meanings in French: "a remainder" in a division problem, "a leftover," "scrap," "residue," etc.

[23] This is a term from French object relations theory.

[24] *Deux*, "two," and *d'eux*, "of or between them," are homonyms in French.

[25] *Sans doute* is not as strong in French as the English "no doubt," which is generally a synonym for "indubitably." *Sans doute* is often better understood to mean *perhaps*.

and dominated by the impossibility of establishing as such, anywhere in the enunciable, the sole One that interests us, the One of the relation "sexual relationship" (rapport sexuel).[26]

That is what analytic discourse demonstrates in that, to one of these beings qua sexed, to man insofar as he is endowed with the organ said to be phallic – I said, "said to be" – the corporal sex (sexe corporel)[27] or sexual organ (sexe) of woman – I said, "of woman," whereas in fact woman does not exist,[28] woman is not whole (pas toute) – woman's sexual organ is of no interest (ne lui dit rien) except via the body's jouissance.

Analytic discourse demonstrates – allow me to put it this way – that the phallus is the conscientious objection made by one of the two sexed beings to the service to be rendered to the other.

Don't talk to me about women's secondary sexual characteristics because, barring some sort of radical change, it is those of the mother that take precedence in her. Nothing distinguishes woman as a sexed being other than her sexual organ (sexe).

Analytic experience attests precisely to the fact that everything revolves around phallic jouissance, in that woman is defined by a position that I have indicated as "not whole" (pas-tout) with respect to phallic jouissance.[29]

I will go a little further. Phallic jouissance is the obstacle owing to which man does not come (n'arrive pas),[30] I would say, to enjoy woman's body, precisely because what he enjoys is the jouissance of the organ.

That is why the superego, which I qualified earlier as based on the (imperative) "Enjoy!", is a correlate of castration, the latter being the sign with which an avowal dresses itself up (se pare), the avowal that jouissance of the Other, of the body of the Other, is promoted only on the basis of

[26] *Rapport* also means "ratio," "proportion," "formula," "relation," "connection," etc.

[27] *Sexe* in French can mean either "sex," in the sense of male or female, or "sexual organ."

[28] Lacan discusses this in detail in Chapters VI and VII; note here simply that, while in French, the emphasis goes on the singular feminine article, *la* of "la femme n'existe pas," in English, saying "*the* woman does not exist" is virtually nonsensical. Lacan is asserting here that Woman with a capital *W*, Woman as singular in essence, does not exist; Woman as an all-encompassing idea (a Platonic form) is an illusion. There is a multiplicity of women, but no essence of "Womanhood" or "Womanliness." *Pas toute*, and *pas-tout* further on, can, in certain instances, be rendered as "not all," but Lacan is not—in my view—primarily concerned here with quantity (all or some). Indeed, he prefers the French term *quanteurs* to *quantificateurs* (for both of which English has only "quantifiers") for the operators presented in Chapters VI and VII.

[29] Lacan uses a spatial metaphor here, *à l'endroit de la jouissance phallique*, which evokes a place. Hence one could literally translate this as "woman is defined by a position that I have indicated as 'not whole' in the place of phallic jouissance." Curiously enough, he says *pas-tout* here instead of *pas-toute*.

[30] While the ostensible meaning here is that "man does not manage to enjoy woman's body," *arriver* is a slang term for "to come" in the sexual sense.

infinity *(de l'infinitude)*.[31] I will say which infinity – that, no more and no less, based on Zeno's paradox.

Achilles and the tortoise, such is the schema of coming *(le schème du jouir)* for one pole *(côté)* of sexed beings.[32] When Achilles has taken his step, gotten it on with Briseis, the latter, like the tortoise,[33] has advanced a bit, because she is "not whole," not wholly his. Some remains. And Achilles must take a second step, and so on and so forth. It is thus that, in our time, but only in our time, we have managed to define numbers – true or, better still, real numbers. Because what Zeno hadn't seen is that the tortoise does not escape the destiny that weighs upon Achilles – its step too gets shorter and shorter and it never arrives at the limit either. It is on that basis that a number, any number whatsoever, can be defined, if it is real. A number has a limit and it is to that extent that it is infinite. It is quite clear that Achilles can only pass the tortoise – he cannot catch up with it. He only catches up with it at infinity *(infinitude)*.

14   Here then is the statement *(le dit)*[34] of the status of jouissance insofar as it is sexual. For one pole,[35] jouissance is marked by the hole that leaves it no other path than that of phallic jouissance. For the other pole, can something be attained that would tell us how that which up until now has only been a fault *(faille)*[36] or gap in jouissance could be realized?

Oddly enough, that is what can only be suggested by very strange glimpses. "Strange" is a word that can be broken down in French – *étrange*, *être-ange*[37] – and that is something that the alternative of being as dumb as the parakeet I mentioned earlier should keep us from falling into. Nevertheless, let us examine more closely what inspires in us the idea that, in the

---

[31] The French here could also be understood as "is promoted (or promotes itself) from infinity" or "from (the vantage point of) the infinite."

[32] As the context shows, it is the male "pole" of sexed beings that is in question here. I have preferred "pole" here to "side" in translating *côté* to emphasize that Lacan is referring to the two poles of sexual differentiation: male and female.

[33] It should be kept in mind here that, in French, the noun *tortue* ("turtle" or "tortoise") is feminine. Regarding Briseis, Achilles' captive mistress, see Homer's *Iliad,* Book I, verse 184 and Book XIX, verses 282–300.

[34] *Le dit* is a very important term in this seminar, and I have resorted to several different ways of translating it in the various contexts in which it appears: "what is said," "the said," "the statement," "the spoken," and so on. It is juxtaposed with *le dire,* another crucial term here, that emphasizes saying, speaking, or enunciating. The French is provided in brackets, except when I translate it as "what is said."

[35] *D'un côté* is often translated, "On the one hand"; here, however, Lacan is referring back to the two "poles" of sexed beings.

[36] *Faille* does not have the moral connotation of "fault" in English, conveying instead the geological meanings of fault – a slip or shift between different land masses or tectonic plates, a point at which things have broken apart. *Faille* also means "lack," "gap," "defect," "break," and "flaw."

[37] *Être-ange:* "angel-being" or "to be an angel."

jouissance of bodies, sexual jouissance has the privilege of being specified by an impasse.

In this space of jouissance, to take something that is limited or closed constitutes a locus, and to speak of it constitutes a topology. In a text soon to be published that is at the cutting edge of my discourse last year, I believe I demonstrate the strict equivalence between topology and structure.[38] If we take that as our guide, what distinguishes anonymity from what we talk about as jouissance – namely, what is regulated by law – is a geometry. A geometry implies the heterogeneity of locus, namely that there is a locus of the Other. Regarding this locus of the Other, of one sex as Other, as absolute Other, what does the most recent development in topology allow us to posit?

I will posit here the term "compactness." Nothing is more compact than a fault, assuming that the intersection of everything that is enclosed therein is accepted as existing over an infinite number of sets, the result being that the intersection implies this infinite number. That is the very definition of compactness.

The intersection I am talking about is the same one I put forward earlier as being that which covers or poses an obstacle to the supposed sexual relationship.

Only "supposed," since I state that analytic discourse is premised solely on the statement that there is no such thing, that it is impossible to found (poser) a sexual relationship. Therein lies analytic discourse's step forward and it is thereby that it determines the real status of all the other discourses.

Named here is the point that covers the impossibility of the sexual relationship as such. Jouissance, qua sexual, is phallic – in other words, it is not related to the Other as such.

Let us follow here the complement of the hypothesis of compactness.

A formulation is given to us by the topology I qualified as the most recent that takes as its point of departure a logic constructed on the investigation of numbers and that leads to the institution of a locus, which is not that of a homogeneous space. Let us take the same limited, closed, supposedly instituted space – the equivalent of what I earlier posited as an intersection extending to infinity. If we assume it to be covered with open sets, in other words, sets that exclude their own limits – the limit is that which is defined as greater than one point and less than another, but in no case equal either to the point of departure or the point of arrival, to sketch it for you quickly – it can be shown that it is equivalent to say that the set of these open spaces

15

[38] Lacan is referring here to his article, "L'Étourdit," published in Scilicet 4 (1973), pp. 5–52.

always allows of a subcovering of open spaces, constituting a finity *(fini-tude)*, namely, that the series of elements constitutes a finite series.

You may note that I did not say that they are countable. And yet that is what the term "finite" implies. In the end, we count them one by one. But before we can count them, we must find an order in them and we cannot immediately assume that that order is findable.

What is implied, in any case, by the demonstrable finity of the open spaces that can cover the space that is limited and closed in the case of sexual jouissance? What is implied is that the said spaces can be taken one by one *(un par un)* – and since I am talking about the other pole, let us put this in the feminine – *une par une*.

That is the case in the space of sexual jouissance, which thereby proves to be compact. The sexed being of these not-whole women does not involve the body but what results from a logical exigency in speech. Indeed, logic, the coherence inscribed in the fact that language exists and that it is outside the bodies that are moved by it – in short, the Other who[39] is incarnated, so to speak, as sexed being – requires this one by one *(une par une)*.

And that is what is strange and, indeed, fascinating, that's the word for it: this requirement of the One, as the *Parmenides* strangely already allowed us to predict, stems from the Other. Where there is being, infinity is required.

I will come back to the status of the Other's locus. But right now I'm going to illustrate it for you, to give you an image of it.

You know how much fun analysts have had with Don Juan, whom they have described in every possible way, including as a homosexual, which really takes the cake. But center him on what I just illustrated for you, this space of sexual jouissance covered by open sets that constitute a finity and that can, in the end, be counted. Don't you see that what is essential in the feminine myth of Don Juan is that he has them one by one *(une par une)?*

That is what the other sex *(l'autre sexe)*,[40] the masculine sex, is for women. In that sense, the image of Don Juan is of capital importance.

From the moment there are names, one can make a list of women and count them. If there are *mille e tre* of them, it's clear that one can take them one by one – that is what is essential. That is entirely different from the One of universal fusion. If woman were not not-whole – if, in her body, she were not not-whole as sexed being – none of that would hold true.

---

[39] It should be kept in mind that French uses the same word, *qui,* for people and things (or abstract entities), whereas English requires us to use either "who" or "that."

[40] In English we would normally speak of the opposite sex, but given the importance in Lacan's work of the other and the Other, I usually prefer the less idiomatic "other sex" for men and "Other sex" for women.

4

The facts I am talking to you about are facts of discourse from which we solicit an exit in analysis – in the name of what? Of letting go of the other discourses.

Through analytic discourse, the subject manifests himself in his gap, namely, in that which causes his desire. Were that not the case, I could not summarize it with a topology that does not involve the same mainspring, the same discourse, but rather a different one, one that is so much purer and that makes so much clearer the fact that there is no genesis except on the basis of discourse. Doesn't the fact that that topology converges with our own experience, to the extent that it allows us to articulate it, justify what, in what I put forward, is lent support and or-worsened *(se s'oupire)* by the fact that it never resorts to any substance, never refers to any being, and breaks with everything smacking of philosophy?[41]

Everything that has been said about being assumes that one can refuse the predicate and say "man is," for example, without saying what. The status of being is closely related to this lopping off of the predicate. Thus, nothing can be said of it except through dead-end detours and demonstrations of logical impossibility, whereby no predicate suffices. As for being *(Ce qui est de l'être)*, a being that would be posited as absolute, it is never anything but the fracture, break, or interruption of the formulation "sexed being," insofar as sexed being is involved *(intéressé)* in jouissance.

November 21, 1972

COMPLEMENT

Beginning of the next class: STUPIDITY *(LA BÊTISE)*.[42]

It seems that in his first "seminar," as it is called, of the year Lacan spoke – I won't beat around the bush – of nothing less than love.

The news has traveled. It even came back to me from – not very far away, of course – a little town in Europe to which it had been sent as a message.

[41] The French here, *d'être en rupture avec quoi que se soit qui s'énonce comme philosophie*, literally means "breaks with anything whatsoever that is enunciated qua philosophy."

[42] *La bêtise* is the term Lacan uses to translate the term Freud instructs little Hans' father to employ to characterize Hans' fear of horses, *Dummheit* (*Gesammelte Werke* VII, p. 263), translated into English as "nonsense" (in *The Standard Edition of the Complete Psychological Works of Sigmund Freud* [New York: Norton, 1955], abbreviated hereafter as SE, followed by volume and page numbers), though it could equally well be rendered in Hans' case as "foolishness" or "funny business" (SE X, p. 28).

As it was from my couch that it came back to me, I cannot believe that the
person who told it to me truly believed it, given that she[43] knows quite well
that what I say of love is assuredly that one cannot speak about it. "Talk to
me of love" – what a lark![44] I spoke of the love letter *(la lettre d'amour)*, of
the declaration of love – not the same thing as the word of love *(la parole
d'amour)*.

I think it is clear, even if you didn't formulate it to yourselves, that in that
first seminar I spoke of stupidity.

At stake is the stupidity that conditions what I named my seminar after
this year and that is pronounced *"encore."* You see the risk involved. I am
only telling you that to show you what constitutes the weight of my presence
here – it's that you enjoy it. My sole presence – at least I dare believe it –
my sole presence in my discourse, my sole presence is my stupidity.[45] I
should know that I have better things to do than to be here *(être là)*.[46] That
is why I might prefer that my presence not be guaranteed to you in each
and every case.

Nevertheless, it is clear that I cannot withdraw, simply say *"encore,"* and
expect it to go on without me *(que ça dure)*. It's stupidity because I myself
obviously collaborate in it. I can only situate myself in the field of this
"encore." Backing up from analytic discourse to what conditions it – namely,
the truth, the only truth that can be indisputable because it is not, that
there's no such thing as a sexual relationship – perhaps doesn't allow one
in any way to judge what is and what is not stupidity. And yet it's impossible, given our experience, not to question something regarding analytic discourse: doesn't this discourse hang together *(se tient)* by basing itself on the
dimension of stupidity?

Why not wonder about the status of this dimension, which is obviously
quite present? After all, there was no need for analytic discourse – therein
lies the subtlety – for the fact that there's no such thing as a sexual relationship to be announced *as truth*.

Don't think I hesitate to get my feet wet. Were I to speak of Saint Paul
today, it would hardly be the first time. That's not what scares me, even if
I compromise myself by discussing people whose status and lineage are not,
strictly speaking, the kind I keep company with. Nevertheless, the fact that
it was the consequence of the Message that men are at one pole *(côté)* and
women at the other has had certain repercussions throughout the ages.

---

[43] The *elle* could just as easily be a "he" here, since it refers back to *personne*,
a feminine noun.
[44] *Parlez-moi d'amour* is the title of a well-known French song from the late
eighteenth or early nineteenth century.
[45] *Présence seule*, which I have translated here as "sole presence," could also
be rendered as "presence alone."
[46] *Être-là* is the French for Dasein.

That hasn't stopped the world from reproducing to the extent of your present numbers. Stupidity is still going strong in any case.

That is not quite the way analytic discourse is established, which I formulated to you as a with S_2 below it,[47] and as what that questions on the side of the subject – in order to produce what, if not stupidity? But, after all, in the name of what would I say that, if it continues, it's stupidity? How is one to get away from stupidity?

It is nevertheless true that there is a status to be granted to this new discourse and to its approach to stupidity. Surely it comes closer, since in other discourses stupidity is what one flees. Discourses always aim at the least stupidity, at sublime stupidity, for "sublime" means the highest point of what lies below.

Where, in analytic discourse, is the sublimity of stupidity? That is what justifies both my giving a rest to my participation in stupidity insofar as it envelopes us here, and my calling on a person who can, on this point, provide me with a response (réplique) based on that which, in other fields, intersects what I say. It is what I had the good fortune to hear, already at the end of last year, from the same person we shall hear from today. He is someone who comes to listen to me here and who is thus sufficiently informed regarding analytic discourse. Right from the beginning of this year, I intend to have him contribute, at his own risk, a response based on what, in a discourse – namely, philosophical discourse – goes its own way, paving it on the basis of a certain status with respect to the least stupidity. I give the floor to François Recanati, whom you already know.

François Recanati's exposé can be found in Scilicet, *the journal of the École freudienne de Paris.*[48]

December 12, 1972

[47] Lacan is referring here to the formula for the analyst's discourse (or analytic discourse) he first elaborates in Seminar XVII:

$$\frac{a}{S_2} \rightarrow \frac{\$}{S_1}$$

The lower right-hand corner is where the *product* of a discourse appears. Lacan is suggesting here that the S_1 produced by analytic discourse is equivalent to stupidity or nonsense *(la bêtise)*. The "side of the subject," mentioned in this sentence, is the right-hand side of the formula. The formula is provided again in the next lecture of the present seminar.

[48] *Scilicet* 4 (1973), pp. 55–73. Recanati had already spoken at Lacan's seminar (Seminar XIX, . . . *ou pire*) on June 14, 1972.

II

To Jakobson

It seems to me that it is difficult not to speak stupidly about language. That is nevertheless what you, Jakobson, manage to do.

Once again, in the talks that Jakobson gave the past few days at the Collège de France,[1] I had the chance to admire him enough to pay homage to him now.

Stupidity nevertheless has to be nourished. Is everything we nourish thereby stupid? No. But it has been demonstrated that to nourish oneself is part and parcel of stupidity. Need I say more to the people present in this room where one is, ultimately, at a restaurant and where one imagines that one is being nourished because one is not at the university cafeteria? One is nourished by the imaginative dimension.

I trust you remember what analytic discourse teaches us about the old bond with the wet nurse, a mother as well, as if by chance, and behind that the infernal business of her desire and everything that follows from it. That is what is at stake in nourishment – some sort of stupidity, but one that analytic discourse puts in its rightful place *(assoit dans son droit)*.

1

One day, I realized that it was difficult not to look into linguistics once the unconscious was discovered.

On the basis of that, I did something that seems to me to be the only true objection I can formulate to what you may have heard the other day from Jakobson's mouth, namely, that all that is language *(tout ce qui est du langage)* falls within the ambit of linguistics – that is, in the final analysis, within the ambit of the linguist.

Not that I don't agree with him about it quite fully when it comes to

[1] The most prestigious French academic institution, located in Paris.

poetry, regarding which he put forward this argument. But if one considers everything that, given the definition of language, follows regarding the foundation of the subject – so thoroughly renewed and subverted by Freud that it is on that basis that everything he claimed to be unconscious can be grounded – then one must, in order to leave Jakobson his own turf *(domaine réservé)*,[2] forge another word. I will call it linguistricks *(linguisterie)*.[3]

That leaves something in my work for the linguist to latch onto, and is not without explaining why I am so often subjected to more than one admonition from so many linguists – certainly not from Jakobson, but that's because he is kindly disposed toward me. In other words, he loves me – that's the way I express it in an intimate context.

The fact that I say *(Mon dire)*[4] that the unconscious is structured like a language is not part and parcel of the field of linguistics. That is a glimpse of what you will see commented upon in a text that will come out in the next issue of my well-known aperiodical *(Scilicet)* and that is entitled *"L'Étourdit,"* that's *d, i, t* at the end[5] – a glimpse of the sentence I wrote on the board several times last year without ever elaborating on it: "The fact that one says remains forgotten behind what is said in what is heard."[6]

Yet, it is in the consequences of what is said that the act of saying is

---

[2] Literally, "private hunting grounds," "game reserve," "private terrain," or "private domain."

[3] From *linguistique* (linguistics). The ending Lacan adds here, *linguisterie*, gives one the impression that it is a kind of specious or fake linguistics. François Raffoul suggested "linguistrickery," which I have shortened to "linguistricks." One could, of course, also see *linguisterie* as a condensation of various other words: *tricherie, strie,* and even *hystérie.*

[4] *Dire,* as a noun, normally refers to one's words, what one says. Here, however, it is not simply a dictum or a statement that is in question but the act of saying itself. As Lacan says in Seminar XIX, it is "qu'on dise comme fait" (June 21, 1972). This sentence could thus be formulated differently: "My saying that the unconscious is structured like a language is not part and parcel of the field of linguistics." Hereafter, I generally translate *le dire* as "the act (or fact) of saying"; when translated otherwise, the French is provided in brackets. The plural, *dires,* does not seem to be used by Lacan in this sense and I have generally translated it as "statements."

[5] *L'Étourdi* (without the final *t,* a homonym of *L'Étourdit*) is the title of a well-known play by Molière; the full title is *L'Étourdi ou les contretemps.* Someone who is *étourdi(e)* is scatterbrained, dizzy, thoughtless, heedless, walks around in a daze, has no idea what is going on, etc. The English translation of Molière's play is aptly entitled *The Blunderer.* By adding a *t* to the end of the word, Lacan creates a condensation involving *étourdi* and *dit* (as a noun, *dit* means "story" or "tale"; more literally, it means "what is said," "the said," or "statement"; as the past participle of the verb *dire,* to say, it means "said"). The construction also suggests that the *étourdi* is *said to be* étourdi, and perhaps only said to be *étourdi* without really being it. The decomposition of the word suggested by the condensation could also include *et* (and), *tour* (trick, tower, or tour), and *dit,* and no doubt other words as well.

[6] The French here does not literally include the words "the fact," relying instead on a subjunctive: *Qu'on dise reste oublié derrière ce qui se dit dans ce qui s'entend* ("That one may say remains forgotten . . ."). Note also the two reflexives and *entendre,* which means both "to hear" and "to understand."

judged. But what one does with what is said remains open. For one can do all kinds of things with it, like one does with furniture when, for example, one is undergoing a siege or a bombardment.

There's a text by Rimbaud that I brought up last year called *"À une raison"* that is scanned by a reply that ends each verse – "A new love" *(Un nouvel amour)*.[7] Since I am supposed to have spoken last time about love, why not take it up again at this level, with the idea once again of indicating the distance between linguistics and linguistricks?

In Rimbaud's text, love is the sign, indicated as such, that one is changing reasons, and that is why the poet addresses that reason. One changes reasons – in other words, one changes discourses.

I will remind you here of the four discourses I distinguished. There are four of them only on the basis of the psychoanalytic discourse that I articulate using four places – each place founded on some effect of the signifier – and that I situate as the last discourse in this deployment. This is not in any sense to be viewed as a series of historical emergences – the fact that one may have appeared longer ago than the others is not what is important here. Well, I would say now that there is some emergence of psychoanalytic discourse whenever there is a movement from one discourse to another.

To apply these categories, which are structured only on the basis of the existence of psychoanalytic discourse, one must pay careful attention to the putting to the test of the truth that there is some emergence of analytic discourse with each shift from one discourse to another. I am not saying anything else when I say that love is the sign that one is changing discourses.

Master's Discourse[8]	*University Discourse*

$$\frac{S_1}{\$} \xrightarrow{\text{impossibility}} \frac{S_2}{a}$$ $$\frac{S_2}{S_1} \xrightarrow{\quad\quad} \underset{\text{impotence}}{} \frac{a}{\$}$$

is clarified by regression from the: is clarified by its "progress" in the:

Hysteric's Discourse	*Analyst's Discourse*

$$\frac{\$}{a} \xrightarrow{\quad\quad} \underset{\text{impotence}}{} \frac{S_1}{S_2}$$ $$\frac{a}{S_2} \xrightarrow{\text{impossibility}} \frac{\$}{S_1}$$

[7] The very short poem entitled *"À une raison"* can be found in Arthur Rimbaud, *Oeuvres complètes* (Paris: Gallimard, 1972), p. 130.

[8] Note that, on at least one occasion, Lacan says that *le discours du maître* can also be understood as the discourse on the master (Seminar XIX, February 3, 1972).

The places are those of:		The terms are:
		S_1, the master signifier
agent	other	S_2, knowledge
———	———	$, the subject
truth	production	a, surplus jouissance

Last time I said that jouissance of the Other is not the sign of love. And here I am saying that love is a sign. Does love consist in the fact that what appears is but the sign?

It is here that the Port-Royal logic, evoked the other day in François Recanati's exposé, could lend us a hand. That logic proposes that the sign – and one always marvels at such statements (dires) that take on weight sometimes long after being pronounced – is what is defined by the disjunction of two substances that have no part in common, namely, by what we nowadays call intersection. That will lead us to some answers a bit later.

What is not a sign of love is jouissance of the Other, jouissance of the Other sex and, as I said, of the body that symbolizes it.

A change of discourses – things budge, things traverse you, things traverse us, things are traversed (ça se traverse), and no one notices the change (personne n'accuse le coup). I can say until I'm blue in the face that the notion of discourse should be taken as a social link (lien social), founded on language, and thus seems not unrelated to what is specified in linguistics as grammar, and yet nothing seems to change.

Perhaps that poses a question that no one raises, that of the status of the notion of information whose success has been so lightning fast that one can say that the whole of science manages to get infiltrated by it. We're at the level of the gene's molecular information and of the winding of nucleoproteins around strands of DNA, that are themselves wrapped around each other, all of that being tied together by hormonal links – that is, messages that are sent, recorded, etc. Let us note that the success of this formula finds its indisputable source in a linguistics that is not only immanent but explicitly formulated. In any case, this action extends right to the very foundations of scientific thought, being articulated as negative entropy.

22

Is that what I, from another locus, that of my linguistricks, gather (recueille) when I make use of the function of the signifier?

2

What is the signifier?

The signifier – as promoted in the rites of a linguistic tradition that is not specifically Saussurian, but goes back as far as the Stoics and is reflected in

Saint Augustine's work – must be structured in topological terms. Indeed, the signifier is first of all that which has a meaning effect *(effet de signifié),*[9] and it is important not to elide the fact that between signifier and meaning effect there is something barred that must be crossed over.[10]

This way of topologizing language's status *(ce qu'il en est du langage)* is illustrated most admirably by phonology, insofar as phonology incarnates the signifier in phonemes. But the signifier cannot in any way be limited to this phonemic prop. Once again – what is a signifier *(qu'est-ce qu'un signifiant)?*

I must already stop, having posed the question in this form.

"A" *(Un),* placed before the term, is usually the indeterminate article.[11] It already assumes that the signifier can be collectivized, that we can make a collection thereof and speak thereof as something that is totalized. Now the linguist would surely have trouble, it seems to me, grounding this collection, grounding it on a "the" *(le),* because there is no predicate that permits that.

As Jakobson pointed out, yesterday as a matter of fact, it is not individual words that can ground the signifier. Words have no other place in which to form a collection than the dictionary, where they can be listed. In order to make you see this, I could speak of sentences, which are clearly signifying units as well, that people sometimes try to collect by selecting sentences that are typical of one language. But instead I will evoke proverbs, in which a certain short article by Paulhan that recently came my way got me more interested.

Paulhan, in the kind of ambiguous dialogue that grabs the attention of the foreigner with a certain limited linguistic competence, noticed that the proverb had a particular weight and played a specific role among the Madagascans. The fact that he discovered it on that occasion does not stop me from going further. Indeed, one can note, in the margins of the proverbial function, that "signifierness" *(signifiance)*[12] is something that fans out *(s'év-*

23

---

[9] The French here, *un effet de signifié,* can also be translated as "an effect as signified" or "the signified qua effect."

[10] Lacan is referring here to his algorithm (a reversal of Saussure's),

$$\frac{S}{s}$$

where "S" designates the signifier and *"s"* designates the signified (i.e., meaning), and the line between the two serves as a bar between the realms of the signifier and the signified. See *Écrits,* 515.

[11] In French, *Un* corresponds both to the indefinite article ("a" in English) and to the number 1. The twofold meaning of *un* must be kept in mind for the whole of the ensuing discussion.

[12] *Signifiance* is an important term that Lacan takes over from linguistics, the French *signifiance* being originally based on the English word "significance." It is taken over by Lacan in the sense that, in linguistics, it merely refers to "the fact of

entaille), if you will allow me this expression, from the proverb to the locution.

Look, for example, in the dictionary under the expression *"à tire-lari-got,"*[13] and you'll see what I mean. Certain dictionaries go so far as to invent a Mr. Larigot: after pulling on his leg over and over, people ended up creating the expression *à tire-larigot*. What does that expression mean? There are plenty of other locutions that are just as extravagant. They mean nothing other than the following – the subversion of desire. That is the meaning of *à tire-larigot*. Through the pierced barrel of signifierness flows *à tire-larigot* a glass, a full glass of signifierness.

What is this signifierness? At the level we are at, it is that which has a meaning effect.

Don't forget that, at the outset, the relationship between signifier and signified was incorrectly qualified as arbitrary. That is how Saussure expressed himself, probably in spite of his better judgment – he certainly believed otherwise, that is, something far closer to the text of the *Cratylus*, as is seen by what he had in his desk drawers, namely, his anagrams. Now what passes for arbitrary is the fact that meaning effects seem not to bear any relation to what causes them.[14]

But if they seem to bear no relation to what causes them, that is because we expect what causes them to bear a certain relation to the real. I'm talking about the serious real. The serious – one must of course make an effort to notice it, one must have come to my seminars now and then – can only be the serial.[15] That can only be obtained after a very long period of extraction, extraction from language of something that is caught up in it, and about

having meaning," whereas in Lacan's work it has to do with the fact of being a signifier (hence the translation I am proposing here: signifierness). When Lacan uses the term, it is to emphasize the nonsensical nature of the signifier, the very existence of signifiers apart from any possible meaning or signification they might have; it is to emphasize the fact that the signifier's very existence exceeds its significatory role, that its substance exceeds its symbolic function, to signify. Thus, rather than referring to "the fact of having meaning," Lacan uses *signifiance* to refer to "the fact of having effects other than meaning effects." We should hear *defiance* in Lacan's *signifiance* – the signifier defies the role allotted to it, refusing to be altogether relegated to the task of signification.

[13] *À tire-larigot* figuratively means "a lot," "in large quantity," "by the bucketful," or "by the shovelful." *Tirer* means to pull. It may be helpful to readers who do not speak French to consider the American expression: "How do you like them apples!" Nothing in the expression itself – that is, none of the individual words or the way in which they are put together – seems to lead up to the meaning "So there!" or "Tough!" that the expression takes on in many contexts. The expression cannot be further decomposed: there are no smaller meaning units within it that create its meaning. The smallest meaning unit here is the whole sentence, which can thus be taken as a single signifying unit or signifier.

[14] For example, the meaning, "a lot" or "by the shovelful," seems to bear no relation to the locution, *à tire larigot*, that is, the signifier that causes it.

[15] *Le sériel*, "what forms a series."

which we have, at the point at which I have arrived in my exposé, only a faint idea – even regarding this indeterminate "a" *(un)*, this lure that we don't know how to make function in relation to the signifier so that it collectivizes the signifier. In truth, we will see that we must turn things around, and instead of investigating *a* signifier *(un signifiant)*, we must investigate the signifier "One" *(Un)* – but we haven't reached that point yet.

Meaning effects seem to bear no relation to what causes them. That means that the references or things the signifier serves to approach remain approximate – macroscopic, for example. What is important is not that it's imaginary – after all, if the signifier allowed us to point to the image we need to be happy, that would be fine and dandy, but it's not the case. At the level of the signifier/signified distinction, what characterizes the relationship between the signified and what serves as the indispensable third party, namely the referent, is precisely that the signified misses the referent. The joiner doesn't work.

24   What really takes the cake is that we nevertheless manage to use it by employing other devices *(trucs)*. To characterize the function of the signifier, to collectivize it in a way that resembles a predication, we have the Port-Royal logic, which is what I began with today. The other day, Recanati mentioned adjectives made into nouns *(substantivés)*.[16] Roundness is extracted from round and – why not? – justice from the just, etc. That is what will allow me to put forward my stupidity *(bêtise)* in order to show that perhaps stupidity is not, as people think, a semantic category, but rather a way of collectivizing the signifier.

Why not? The signifier is stupid.

It seems to me that this could lead to a smile, a stupid smile, naturally. A stupid smile, as everyone knows – it suffices to visit cathedrals – is an angel's smile.[17] Indeed, that is the only justification for Pascal's warning *(semonce)*.[18] If an angel has such a stupid smile, that is because it is up to its ears in the supreme signifier. To find itself on dry land would do it some good – perhaps it wouldn't smile anymore.

It's not that I believe in angels – as everyone knows, I believe in them inextricably and even "inex-Teilhard-ly"[19] – it's just that I don't believe

[16] In French, *un substantif* is a noun.
[17] Lacan is evidently referring here to the statue *L'Ange au Sourire* (the Smiling Angel), the guardian angel of Saint Nicaise, at the Cathédrale de Reims, dating back to the thirteenth century.
[18] Is it an accident that the term Lacan selects here, *semonce*, is of juridical origin and was also made into a noun? See Lacan's favorite dictionary, *Dictionnaire étymologique de la langue française*, Bloch and von Wartburg (Paris: Presses Universitaires de France, 1932).
[19] *Inextrayablement* and *inexteilhardement* sound more similar in French than do the terms I have used here to translate them: "inextricably" and "inex-Teilhard-

they bear the slightest message, and it is in that respect that they are truly signifying.

Why do I so strongly emphasize the function of the signifier? Because it is the foundation of the symbolic dimension that only analytic discourse allows us to isolate as such.

I could have approached things in another way – by telling you, for example, how people go about asking me to be their analyst.

I don't want to spoil such pristine purity. Certain people would recognize themselves – God knows what they might imagine I think. Perhaps they would believe that I think they are stupid. That is truly the last thing that would cross my mind in such a case. The question of import here concerns the fact that analytic discourse introduces an adjective made into a noun, "stupidity," insofar as it is a dimension of the signifier at work *(une dimension en exercice du signifiant)*.

Here we must take a closer look.

3

As soon as we turn things into nouns, we presuppose a substance, and nowadays, well, we just don't have that many substances. We have thinking substance and extended substance.[20]

On that basis, it would perhaps be appropriate to ask where the "substantial" dimension can be situated – however far it may be from us and, heretofore, giving but a sign to us *(ne nous faisant que signe)* – this substance at work *(en exercice)*, this dimension that should be written "dit-mension,"[21] over which the function of language is first of all that which is watchful, prior to any more rigorous use. 25

First of all, it can be said that we have changed thinking substance considerably. Since the "I am thinking"[22] that, presupposing itself, grounds existence, we have had to take a step – that of the unconscious.

Since today I'm dragging my feet in the rut of the unconscious structured like a language, it should be realized that this formulation totally changes the function of the subject as existing. The subject is not the one *(celui)*

___

ly." Pierre Teilhard de Chardin (1881–1955) was a French Christian theologian and philosopher.
   [20] *Res cogitans* and *res extensa*.
   [21] *Dit* (the *t* is silent) means "what is said"; here Lacan is suggesting that it is a dimension of the said or spoken. *Mension* combines the homonyms *mansion* (from the Latin *mansio* [dwelling], which in French was the term for each part of a theater set in the Middle Ages), and *mention* (mention, note, or honors, as in *cum laude*).
   [22] See the most recent English translation of Descartes' *Philosophical Writings* by J. Cottingham (Cambridge: Cambridge University Press, 1986): "I am thinking, therefore I am."

who thinks. The subject is precisely the one we encourage, not to say it all *(tout dire)*,[23] as we tell him in order to charm him – one cannot say it all – but rather to utter stupidities. That is the key.

For it is with those stupidities that we do analysis, and that we enter into the new subject – that of the unconscious. It is precisely to the extent that the guy is willing not to think anymore that we will perhaps learn a little bit more about it, that we will draw certain consequences from his words *(dits)* – words that cannot be taken back *(se dédire)*, for that is the rule of the game.

From that emerges a speaking *(dire)* that does not always go so far as to be able to "ex-sist" with respect to the words spoken *(ex-sister au dit)*.[24] That is because of what gets included in those words as a consequence thereof.[25] That is the acid-test *(épreuve)* by which, in analyzing anyone, no matter how stupid, a certain real may be reached.

The status of the saying *(dire)* – I must leave all of that aside for today. But I can announce to you that an even bigger pain in the ass for us this year will be to put to this test *(épreuve)* a certain number of sayings *(dires)* from the philosophical tradition.

Fortunately, Parmenides actually wrote poems. Doesn't he use linguistic devices[26] – the linguist's testimony takes precedence here – that closely resemble mathematical articulation, alternation after succession, framing after alternation? It is precisely because he was a poet that Parmenides says what he has to say to us in the least stupid of manners. Otherwise, the idea that being is and that nonbeing is not, I don't know what that means to you, but personally I find that stupid. And you mustn't believe that it amuses me to say so.

Nevertheless, we will, this year, need being and the signifier One *(Un)*, for which I paved the way last year by saying – "There's such a thing as

[23] *Tout dire,* to say it all or to say everything, is a common French rendering of Freud's "say whatever comes to mind."

[24] The expression Lacan uses here, *ex-sister au dit,* is not easily rendered in English; Lacan is borrowing a term, *ex-sistence,* which was first introduced into French in translations of Heidegger's work (e.g., *Being and Time*), as a translation for the Greek εκστασις and the German *Ekstase.* The root meaning of the term in Greek is "standing outside of" or "standing apart from" something. In Greek, it was generally used for the removal or displacement of something, but it also came to be applied to states of mind that we would now call "ecstatic." (Thus, a derivative meaning of the word is "ecstasy.") Heidegger often played on the root meaning of the word, "standing outside" or "stepping outside oneself," but also on its close connection in Greek with the root of the word for "existence." Lacan uses it to talk about an existence that stands apart, which insists as it were from the outside, something not included on the inside. Rather than being intimate, it is "extimate."

[25] The meaning of Lacan's sentence here is very unclear: *A cause de ce qui vient au dit comme conséquence.*

[26] *Des appareils de langage:* literally, "language apparatuses" or "linguistic apparatuses."

One!" *(Y a d' l'Un!)* For it is there that the serious begins, as stupid as that too may seem. Thus, we'll have several references to take up in the philosophical tradition.

We can't get rid of that renowned extended substance, the complement of that other substance, that easily either, since it is modern space – the substance of pure space, like we say "pure spirit." It certainly isn't very promising.

Pure space is based on the notion of the part, as long as one adds to that the following, that all of the parts are external to each other – *partes extra partes*. People managed to extract a few little things from even that, but some serious steps had to be taken.

26

In order to situate my signifier before leaving you today, I will ask you to consider what was inscribed at the beginning of my first sentence last time – "enjoying a body" *(jouir d'un corps)*, a body that symbolizes the Other[27] – as it perhaps involves something that can help us focus on another form of substance, enjoying substance *(la substance jouissante)*.

Isn't that precisely what psychoanalytic experience presupposes? – the substance of the body, on the condition that it is defined only as that which enjoys itself *(se jouit)*. That is, no doubt, a property of the living body, but we don't know what it means to be alive except for the following fact, that a body is something that enjoys itself *(cela se jouit)*.

It enjoys itself only by "corporizing" *(corporiser)*[28] the body in a signifying way. That implies something other than the *partes extra partes* of extended substance. As is emphasized admirably by the kind of Kantian that Sade was, one can only enjoy a part of the Other's body, for the simple reason that one has never seen a body completely wrap itself around the Other's body, to the point of surrounding and phagocytizing it. That is why we must confine ourselves to simply giving it a little squeeze, like that, taking a forearm or anything else – ouch!

Enjoying *(jouir)* has the fundamental property that it is, ultimately, one person's body that enjoys a part of the Other's body.[29] But that part also enjoys – the Other likes it more or less, but it is a fact that the Other cannot remain indifferent to it.

Occasionally something even happens that goes beyond what I just described, and that is marked by utter signifying ambiguity – for the expression "enjoyment of the body" *(jouir du corps)* includes a genitive that has a certain Sadian flavor to it, as I've mentioned, or, on the contrary, an

---

[27] Lacan does not quote himself exactly here.
[28] The French *corporiser* (more commonly *corporifier*) means to give a body to that which is spirit or to give a solid consistency to a fluid.
[29] More literally stated, it is "the body of the one that enjoys a part of the body of the Other."

ecstatic, subjective flavor suggesting, in fact, that it is the Other who enjoys.[30]

As concerns jouissance, that is but an elementary level. The last time, I put forward the notion that jouissance is not a sign of love. That is what I shall have to argue for, and it will lead us to the level of phallic jouissance. But what I, strictly speaking, call "jouissance of the Other," insofar as it is merely symbolized here, is something else altogether – namely, the not-whole that I will have to articulate.

4

In this single articulation, what is the signifier – the signifier for today, and to close on this point, given the motives I have regarding it?

I will say that the signifier is situated at the level of enjoying substance *(substance jouissante)*. That is completely different from Aristotelian physics, which I am about to discuss, and which, precisely because it can be used *(sollicitée)* in the way I am going to use it, shows us to what extent it was illusory.

The signifier is the cause of jouissance. Without the signifier, how could we even approach that part of the body?[31] Without the signifier, how could we center that something that is the material cause of jouissance?[32] However fuzzy or confused it may be, it is a part of the body that is signified in this contribution *(apport)*.

Now I will go right to the final cause, final in every sense of the term because it is the terminus – the signifier is what brings jouissance to a halt.

After those who embrace *(s'enlacent)* – if you'll allow me – alas *(hélas)!* And after those who are weary *(las)*,[33] hold on there *(holà)!* The other pole of the signifier, its stopping action *(coup d'arrêt)*, is as much there *(est là)* at the origin as the commandment's direct addressing *(vocatif)* can be.

The efficient, which Aristotle proposes as the third form of the cause, is nothing in the end but the project through which jouissance is limited. All kinds of things that appear in the animal kingdom make a parody of speaking beings' path to jouissance, while simultaneously sketching out message-like functions – for example, the bee transporting the pollen of the male

---

[30] The genitive here, *de* (combined here with *le* to form *du*), can, as Lacan says in "Subversion of the Subject and Dialectic of Desire" (*Écrits*, 814), be objective (e.g., I derive enjoyment *from* the Other's body) or subjective (e.g., the Other's body enjoys).

[31] That is, "that part of the body" discussed five paragraphs back or, more simply, "a part of the body."

[32] On the four Aristotelian causes, see also "Science and Truth" in *Écrits*.

[33] *Las* is also a very old French term for "alas."

flower to the female flower closely resembles what goes on in communication.

And the embrace *(l'étreinte)*, the confused embrace wherein jouissance finds its cause, its last cause, which is formal – isn't it something like grammar that commands it?

It's no accident that Pierre beats Paul at the crux of the first examples of (French) grammar, nor that – why not put it this way? – Pierre and Paule *(Pierre et Paule)* constitute the example of conjunction, except that one must wonder, afterwards, who shoves *(épaule)* the other. I've already gotten a lot of mileage out of that one.

One could even say that the verb is defined as a signifier that is not as stupid – you have to write that as one word – *notasstupid* as the others, no doubt, providing as it does the movement of a subject to his own division in jouissance, and it is all the less stupid when the verb determines this division as disjunction, and it becomes a sign.

Last year I played on a slip of the pen I made in a letter addressed to a woman – *tu ne sauras jamais combien je t'ai aimé* ("you will never know how much I loved you") – *é* instead of *ée*.[34] Since then, someone mentioned to me that that could mean that I am a homosexual. But what I articulated quite precisely last year is that when one loves, it has nothing to do with sex.

That is what I would like to end with today, if you will.

December 19, 1972

[34] The past participle, *aimé,* is supposed to agree in gender with the sex of the person designated in the phrase by the direct object, *te* (here *t'*); if the person is male, the participle remains *aimé,* if female, an *e* should be added to the end: *aimée.*

III

The function of the written[1]

THE UNCONSCIOUS IS WHAT IS READ.

ON THE USE OF LETTERS.

S/s.

ONTOLOGY, THE MASTER'S DISCOURSE.

SPEAKING OF FUCKING.

THE UNREADABLE.

I am going to enter very slowly into what I have reserved for you today, which, before beginning, strikes me as rather reckless. It has to do with the way in which we must situate the function of the written in analytic discourse.

There is an anecdote to be related here, namely, that one day, on the cover of a collection I brought out – *poubellication,* as I called it[2] – I found nothing better to write than the word *Écrits.*

It is rather well known that those *Écrits* cannot be read easily. I can make a little autobiographical admission – that is exactly what I thought. I thought, perhaps it goes that far, I thought they were not meant to be read.

That's a good start.

1

A letter is something that is read.[3] It even seems to be designed as a sort of extension *(prolongement)* of the word. It is read *(ça se lit)* and literally at that. But it is not the same thing to read a letter as it is to read. It is quite clear that, in analytic discourse, what is involved is but that – that which is read, that which is read beyond what you have incited the subject to say, which, as I emphasized the last time, is not so much to say everything[4]

---

[1] What I am translating here as "the written" is *"l'écrit"* which can also mean writing, a text (as in Lacan's *Écrits,* i.e., his writings), etc. It is not always easily distinguished here from *écriture,* writing, but should not be confused with the act or fact of writing, as it refers specifically to that which *has already been* written. In the few cases in which I render it as "writing," I provide the French in brackets.

[2] *Poubellication* is a condensation of *poubelle,* garbage can (or dustbin), and *publication,* publication. It can perhaps also be seen to contain *embellir,* to beautify, and other words as well.

[3] Or "A letter is something that can be read" or "A letter is something you read": *La lettre, ça se lit.*

[4] In the context of the last chapter, I translated this *tout dire* as to "say it all."

as to say anything, without worrying about saying something stupid *(des bêtises)*.

That assumes that we develop the dimension [of stupidity], but it cannot be developed without the act of saying.[5] What is the dimension of stupidity? Stupidity, at least the stupidity one can proffer, doesn't go far. In common discourse, it stops short.

That is what I check when I look back, which I never do without trembling, at what I have proffered in the past. That always makes me awfully afraid, afraid of having said something stupid, in other words, something that, due to what I am now putting forward, I might consider not to hold up.

Thanks to someone who is writing up this Seminar – the first year at the *École normale* will be coming out soon[6] – I was able to get the sense, which I encounter sometimes when put to the test, that what I put forward that year was not as stupid as all that, and at least wasn't so stupid as to have stopped me from putting forward other things that seem to me, because that's where I'm at now, to hold water.

Nevertheless, this "rereading oneself" *(se relire)* represents a dimension that must be situated in relation to what is, with respect to analytic discourse, the function of that which is read *(ce qui se lit)*.

Analytic discourse has a privilege in this regard. That is what I began from in what constitutes a crucial date for me in what I am teaching – it is perhaps not so much on the "I" that emphasis must be placed, namely, concerning what "I" can proffer, as on the "from" *(de)*, in other words, on from whence comes the teaching of which I am the effect. Since then, I have grounded analytic discourse on the basis of a precise articulation, which can be written on the blackboard with four letters, two bars, and five lines that connect up each of the letters two by two. One of these lines – since there are four letters, there should be six lines – is missing.

This writing *(écriture)*[7] stemmed from an initial reminder, namely, that analytic discourse is a new kind of relation based only on what functions as speech, in something one may define as a field. "Function and Field," I wrote, "of Speech and Language," I ended, "in Psychoanaly-

30

---

[5] *Sans le dire* could also mean "without saying so."

[6] Lacan is referring here to Seminar XI, published in English as *The Four Fundamental Concepts of Psychoanalysis* (New York: Norton, 1978). The text was edited by Jacques-Alain Miller and published by *Éditions du Seuil* in 1973.

[7] In English, we would normally refer to the kind of symbolism Lacan refers to here (the analyst's discourse whose written formulation was given in Chapter II) and also later in this chapter as *notation* or *symbols,* not as a writing, much less as *a* written or what is written. Given, however, Lacan's discussion in this chapter, I have opted to stretch the English use of the words writing and written, rather than always strive for the best-sounding English translation. Lacan himself uses the term "notation" later in this chapter.

sis"[8] – that amounted to designating what constitutes the originality of this discourse, which is not the same as a certain number of others that serve specific purposes *(qui font office)*, and that, due to this very fact, I qualify as official discourses *(discours officiels)*. The point is to discern the purpose *(office)* of analytic discourse, and to render it, if not official, at least officiating.

It is in this discourse that we must indicate what the function of the written in analytic discourse may be, if it is, indeed, specific.

To allow for the explanation of the functions of this discourse, I put forward the use of a certain number of letters. First of all, *a*, which I call "object," but which, nevertheless, is but a letter. Then A,[9] that I make function in that aspect of the proposition that takes only the form of a written formula,[10] and that is produced by mathematical logic. I designate thereby that which is first of all a locus, a place. I called it "the locus of the Other" *(le lieu de l'Autre)*.[11]

In what respect can a letter serve to designate a locus? It is clear that there is something that is not quite right here. When you open, for example, to the first page of what was finally collected in the form of a definitive edition entitled *Theory of Sets*,[12] bearing the name of a fictitious author, Nicolas Bourbaki, what you see is the putting into play of a certain number of logical signs. One of them designates the function of "place" as such. It is written as a little square: □.

Thus, I wasn't making a strict use of the letter when I said that the locus of the Other was symbolized by the letter A. On the contrary, I marked it by redoubling it with the S that means signifier here, signifier of A insofar as the latter is barred: S($\cancel{A}$). I thereby added a dimension to A's locus, showing that qua locus it does not hold up, that there is a fault, hole, or loss therein. Object *a* comes to function with respect to that loss. That is something which is quite essential to the function of language.

Lastly, I used the letter Φ, to be distinguished from the merely signifying function that had been promoted in analytic theory up until then with the

[8] This is the title of Lacan's well-known Rome discourse from 1953 included in *Écrits*.
[9] In this Seminar (as elsewhere), I adopt the French convention of using A for Other *(Autre)* instead of O, because the barred Other, when written Ø, is easily confused with the empty set, {Ø}.
[10] The French here strikes me as somewhat ambiguous: *ce qui de la proposition n'a pris que formule écrite*.
[11] This could also be translated as "the Other's locus" or "the Other as locus."
[12] Originally published in French as *Éléments de mathématique, Théorie des ensembles* (Paris: Hermann), it was translated into English and published as *Elements of Mathematics: Theory of Sets* (Reading: Addison-Wesley, 1968).

term "phallus." It is something original whose true import I am specifying today as being indicated by its very writing.[13]

If these three letters are different, it is because they do not have the same function.

To once again take up the thread of analytic discourse, we must now discern what these letters introduce into the function of the signifier.

2

The written is in no way in the same register or made of the same stuff, if you'll allow me this expression, as the signifier.

The signifier is a dimension that was introduced by linguistics. Linguistics, in the field in which speech is produced, is not self-evident *(ne va pas de soi).*[14] A discourse sustains it, which is scientific discourse. Linguistics introduces into speech a dissociation thanks to which the distinction between signifier and signified is grounded. It divides up what seems to be self-evident, which is that when one speaks, one's speech signifies, bringing with it the signified, and, still further, is only based, up to a certain point, on the function of signification.

Distinguishing the dimension of the signifier only takes on importance when it is posited that what you hear, in the auditory sense of the term, bears no relation whatsoever to what it signifies. That is an act that is instituted only through a discourse, scientific discourse. And it is not self-evident. Indeed, it is so scarcely self-evident that a whole discourse – which does not flow from a bad pen, since it is the *Cratylus,* by none other than Plato – results from the endeavor to show that there must be a relationship and that the signifier in and of itself means something. This attempt, which we can qualify from our vantage point as desperate, is marked by failure, because another discourse, scientific discourse, due to its very institution – in a way whose history we need not probe here – gives us the following, that the signifier is posited only insofar as it has no relation to the signified.   32

The very terms we use to talk about it are still slippery. A linguist as discerning as Ferdinand de Saussure speaks of arbitrariness. That is tantamount to slipping, slipping into another discourse, the master's discourse, to call a spade a spade. Arbitrariness is not a suitable term here.

When we develop a discourse, if we are to remain within its field and not

[13] Lacan's phraseology is quite complicated here: *que je spécifie aujourd'hui d'être précisé dans son relief par l'écrit même.*
[14] The expression Lacan uses here, *aller de soi,* variants of which are repeated throughout the next few paragraphs, can generally be translated as "to be self-evident," but more literally means to "go it alone," "stand alone," or "require no outside support." Here linguistics is sustained by *another* discourse, scientific discourse.

fall back into another, we must always try to give it its own consistency and not step outside of it except advisedly. This vigilance is all the more necessary when what is at stake is what constitutes a discourse *(quand il s'agit de ce qu'est un discours)*. To say that the signifier is arbitrary does not have the same import as to simply say that it bears no relation to its meaning effect, for the former involves slipping into another reference.

The word "reference," in this case, can only be situated on the basis of what discourse constitutes by way of a link *(lien)*. The signifier as such refers to nothing if not to a discourse, in other words, a mode of functioning or a utilization of language qua link.

We must still indicate here what this link means. The link – we can but turn to this right away – is a link between those who speak. You can immediately see where we are headed – it's not just anyone who speaks, of course; it's beings, beings we are used to qualifying as "living," and it would, perhaps, be rather difficult to exclude the dimension of life from those who speak. But we immediately realize that this dimension simultaneously brings in that of death, and that a radical signifying ambiguity results from this. The sole function on the basis of which life can be defined, namely, the reproduction of a body, can itself be characterized neither by life nor by death, since reproduction as such, insofar as it is sexual *(sexuée)*, involves both life and death.

Already, by merely swimming with the tide of analytic discourse, we have made a jump known as a "world view" *(conception du monde)*, which to us must nevertheless be the funniest thing going. The term "world view" supposes a discourse – that of philosophy – that is entirely different from ours.

If we leave behind philosophical discourse, nothing is less certain than the existence of a world. One can only laugh when one hears people claim that analytic discourse involves something on the order of such a conception.

I would go even further – putting forward such a term to designate Marxism is also a joke. Marxism does not seem to me to be able to pass for a world view. The statement of what Marx says *(L'énoncé de ce que dit Marx)* runs counter to that in all sorts of striking ways. Marxism is something else, something I will call a gospel. It is the announcement that history is instating another dimension of discourse and opening up the possibility of completely subverting the function of discourse as such and of philosophical discourse, strictly speaking, insofar as a world view is based upon the latter.

Generally speaking, language proves to be a field much richer in resources than if it were merely the field in which philosophical discourse has inscribed itself over the course of time. But certain reference points have been enunciated by that discourse that are difficult to completely eliminate from any use of language. That is why there is nothing easier than to fall back into what I ironically called a world view, but which has a more moderate and more precise name: ontology.

Ontology is what highlighted in language the use of the copula, isolating it as a signifier.[15] To dwell on the verb "to be" – a verb that is not even, in the complete field of the diversity of languages, employed in a way we could qualify as universal – to produce it as such is a highly risky enterprise.

In order to exorcise it, it might perhaps suffice to suggest that when we say about anything whatsoever that it is what it is, nothing in any way obliges us to isolate the verb "to be." That is pronounced "it is what it is" *(c'est ce que c'est)*, and it could just as well be written, "idizwadidiz" *(seskecé)*. In this use of the copula, we would see nothing at all. We would see nothing whatsoever if a discourse, the discourse of the master, *m'être*,[16] didn't emphasize the verb "to be" *(être)*.

That is what Aristotle himself thinks about twice before propounding since, to designate the being he juxtaposes to τὸ τί ἐστι, that is, to quiddity or what it is, he goes so far as to employ the following, τὸ τί ἦν εἶναι – what would have happened if that which was to be had simply come to be.[17] It seems that the pedicle[18] is conserved here that allows us to situate from whence this discourse on being is produced – it's quite simply being at someone's heel, being at someone's beck and call – what would have been if you had understood what I ordered you to do.[19]

---

[15] *Comme signifiant* could also mean "as signifying."

[16] *Maître*, "master," and *m'être* are generally pronounced identically in French. The latter literally means "to be myself," but in certain expressions – e.g., *je me souviens de m'être aperçu que . . .* "I recall having noticed that . . ." – it is simply part and parcel of a reflexive construction.

Lacan's discussion here is continued in Seminar XXI (*Les non-dupes errent*, January 15, 1974), where Lacan says, " '[S]peaking being' . . . is a pleonasm, because there is only being due to speaking; were it not for the verb 'to be,' there would be no being at all."

[17] The Greek expressions here can be found in many passages in Aristotle's *Metaphysics;* see, for example, Book V, Chapter 18, 1022a25–27, where τὸ τί ἦν εἶναι is translated by W. D. Ross as "what it was to be." (Richard Hope translates it as "what it means to be.") Ross more generally translates it as "essence." Lacan's French here reads as follows: *ce qui se serait produit si était venu à être, tout court, ce qui était à être.* This could also be rendered: "what would have been produced if that which should have been had come into Being."

[18] The *pédicule* ("pedicle," "pedicel," or "peduncle") – a term that has many meanings in anatomy, botany, and zoology, and whose root is *pes*, "foot" – in question here is most likely the Greek word ἦν (if or unless), which is often used in subjunctive clauses and as part of a negation (with μή). It is thus similar to the French *ne* when used as an "expletive" (for example, in *craindre qu'il ne vienne*), which Lacan discusses in great detail in Seminar IX, *Identification*. See also Lacan's use of *pédicule* in Seminar XIX (March 15, 1972).

[19] The French here is far more polyvalent: *c'est tout simplement l'être à la botte, l'être aux ordres, ce qui allait être si tu avais entendu ce que je t'ordonne.* The *allait être* involves an imperfect tense, and Lacan often plays on the French imperfect, since it

Every dimension of being is produced in the wake of the master's discourse – the discourse of he who, proffering the signifier, expects therefrom one of its link effects that must not be neglected, which is related to the fact that the signifier commands. The signifier is, first and foremost, imperative.

How is one to return, if not on the basis of a peculiar *(spécial)* discourse, to a prediscursive reality? That is the dream – the dream behind every conception *(idée)* of knowledge. But it is also what must be considered mythical. There's no such thing as a prediscursive reality. Every reality is founded and defined by a discourse.

That is why it is important for us to realize what analytic discourse is made of, and not to misrecognize the following, which no doubt has but a limited place therein, that we speak in analytic discourse about what the verb "to fuck" *(foutre)* enunciates perfectly well. We speak therein of fucking,[20] and we say that it's not working out *(ça ne va pas).*[21]

34   That is an important part of what is confided in analytic discourse, but it is worth highlighting that analytic discourse does not have exclusivity in this regard. For that is also what is expressed in what I earlier referred to as "current discourse" *(discours courant).* Let us write that as *"disque-ourcourant"* [pronounced in the same way as *discours courant,* but *disque* means record or disk], *disque aussi hors-champ, hors jeu de tout discours* [a disk that is also or so very outside of the field, out of the game, or beyond the rules of all discourse], *donc disque tout court* [thus, just a disk] – it goes around and around for nothing, quite precisely. The disk is found in the very field on the basis of which all discourses are specified and where they all drown, where each and every one of them is just as capable of enunciating as much of the field as the others, but due to a concern with what I will call, for very good reasons, "decency" *(décence),*[22] does so – well – as little as possible.

What constitutes the basis of life, in effect, is that for everything having to do with the relations between men and women, what is called collectivity, it's not working out *(ça ne va pas).* It's not working out, and the whole world talks about it, and a large part of our activity is taken up with saying so.

Nevertheless, there is nothing serious if not what is organized in another way as discourse. That includes the fact that this relationship, this sexual

can mean what "was going to be," "was about to be," or "would have been" if. . . . The French thus moves from an imperfect to a pluperfect *(avais entendu,* meaning "heard" or "understood," and perhaps even "heeded" or "agreed to" here) and then to a present tense (what I "order" or "am ordering" you to do).
    [20] In the French, Lacan specifies here that he is talking about the verb form of *foutre* by referring to the English verb, "to fuck"; as a noun, *foutre* means "cum."
    [21] This elementary French expression can be translated in a number of other ways as well: "it's no good," "it's not going well," etc.
    [22] *Décence* is a homonym for *des sens,* meanings.

relationship, insofar as it's not working out, works out anyway *(il va quand même)* – thanks to a certain number of conventions, prohibitions, and inhibitions that are the effect of language and can only be taken from that fabric and register. There isn't the slightest prediscursive reality, for the very fine reason that what constitutes a collectivity – what I called men, women, and children – means nothing qua prediscursive reality. Men, women, and children are but signifiers.

A man is nothing but a signifier. A woman seeks out a man qua signifier *(au titre de signifiant)*. A man seeks out a woman qua – and this will strike you as odd – that which can only be situated through discourse, since, if what I claim is true – namely, that woman is not-whole – there is always something in her that escapes discourse.

3

What we need to know is what, in a discourse, is produced by the effect of the written. As you perhaps know – you know it in any case if you read what I write – the fact that linguistics has distinguished the signifier and the signified is not the whole story. Perhaps that seems self-evident to you. But it is precisely by considering things to be self-evident that we see nothing of what is right before our eyes, before our eyes concerning the written. Linguistics has not simply distinguished the signified from the signifier. If there is something that can introduce us to the dimension of the written as such, it is the realization that the signified has nothing to do with the ears, but only with reading – the reading of the signifiers we hear.[23] The signified is not what you hear. What you hear is the signifier. The signified is the effect of the signifier.

One can distinguish here something that is but the effect of discourse, of discourse as such – in other words, of something that already functions qua link. Let us take things at the level of a writing *(un écrit)* that is itself the effect of a discourse, scientific discourse, namely the writing *(l'écrit)* S, designed to connote the place of the signifier, and *s* with which the signified is connoted as a place. Place as a function is created only by discourse itself. "Places everyone!"[24] – that functions only in discourse. Anyway, between the two, S and *s*, there is a bar, $\frac{S}{s}$.

35

---

[23] The French here is *la lecture de ce qu'on entend de signifiant*, which can be translated literally as, "the reading of what one hears qua signifier (or qua signifying)"; the sentences that follow in the text are what allow for the translation I have provided there.
[24] The French here, *chacun à sa place*, literally means "everyone in his place."

It doesn't look like anything when you write a bar in order to explain things. This word, "explain," is of the utmost importance because there ain't nothing you can understand in a bar, even when it is reserved for signifying negation.[25]

It is very difficult to understand what negation means. If you look at it a bit closely, you realize in particular that there is a wide variety of negations that it is quite impossible to cover with the same concept. The negation of existence, for example, is not at all the same as the negation of totality.[26]

There is something that is even more certain: adding a bar to the notation S and s is already a bit superfluous and even futile, insofar as what it brings out is already indicated by the distance of what is written.[27] The bar, like everything involving what is written, is based only on the following – what is written is not to be understood.

That is why you are not obliged to understand my writings. If you don't understand them, so much the better – that will give you the opportunity to explain them.

It's the same with the bar. The bar is precisely the point at which, in every use of language, writing *(l'écrit)* may be produced. If, in Saussure's work itself, S is above s, that is, over the bar, it is because the effects of the unconscious have no basis without this bar – that is what I was able to show you in "The Instance of the Letter," included in my *Écrits*, in a way that is written *(qui s'écrit)*, nothing more.

Indeed, were it not for this bar nothing about language could be explained by linguistics. Were it not for this bar above which there are signifiers that pass, you could not see that signifiers are injected into the signified.[28]

Were there no analytic discourse, you would continue to speak like bird-brains, singing the "current disk" *(disque-ourcourant),*[29] making the disk go around, that disk that turns because "there's no such thing as a sexual relationship" – a formulation that can only be articulated thanks to the entire

[25] See Chapter VII, where Lacan uses a bar over the different "quantifiers" to signify negation.

[26] See Chapter VII, where Lacan introduces the existential and universal quantifiers.

[27] Presumably, the distance between the S and s in the notation $\frac{S}{s}$.

[28] Lacan's French here, *vous ne pourriez voir que du signifiant s'injecte dans le signifié,* is rendered a bit odd because Lacan doesn't say a signifier or several signifiers, but rather some signifier, in the sense in which we speak in English about "some bread" or "some water," in other words, as an unquantifiable substance. Here, signifier is injected into the signified, apparently like fuel is injected into an engine.

[29] "Disk" *(disque)* should be understood here primarily in the sense of a phonograph record.

edifice of analytic discourse, and that I have been drumming into you for quite some time.

But drumming it into you, I must nevertheless explain it – it is based only on the written in the sense that the sexual relationship cannot be written *(ne peut pas s'écrire)*. Everything that is written stems from the fact that it will forever be impossible to write, as such, the sexual relationship. It is on that basis that there is a certain effect of discourse, which is called writing.

One could, at a pinch, write *x R y*, and say *x* is man, *y* is woman, and *R* is the sexual relationship. Why not? The only problem is that it's stupid, because what is based on the signifier function *(la fonction de signifiant)*[30] of "man" and "woman" are mere signifiers that are altogether related to the "curcurrent" *(courcourant)*[31] use of language. If there is a discourse that demonstrates that to you, it is certainly analytic discourse, because it brings into play the fact that woman will never be taken up except *quoad matrem*. Woman serves a function in the sexual relationship only qua mother.

Those are overall truths *(vérités massives)*, but they will lead us further. Thanks to what? Thanks to writing. Writing will not object to this first approximation since it is in this way that writing will show that woman's jouissance is based on a supplementation of this not-whole *(une suppléance de ce pas-toute)*. She finds the cork[32] for this jouissance [based on the fact] that she is not-whole[33] – in other words, that makes her absent from herself somewhere, absent as subject – in the *a* constituted by her child.

As for *x* – in other words, what man would be if the sexual relationship could be written in a sustainable way, a way that is sustainable in a discourse – man is but a signifier because where he comes into play as a signifier, he comes in only *quoad castrationem*, in other words, insofar as he has a relation to phallic jouissance. The upshot being that as soon as a discourse, analytic discourse, seriously took up this question and posited that the precondition of what is written is that it be sustained by a discourse, everything fell apart. Now you'll never be able to write the sexual relationship – write

[30] This ambiguous expression could also arguably be translated as "signifying function" or "function as signifier."
[31] *Courcourant* involves a doubling of the first syllable of *courant*, "current" (in all senses of the term), making it a bit singsong-like. *Cour* alone is courtyard, also suggesting that this is a courtyard or backyard use of language. *Cou cou* is a sound birds (or birdbrains?) make in French, and a *coucou* is a cuckoo (bird or clock). *Coucou* is also what you say to a little baby to say "peek-a-boo!" *Courant* means running, giving the additional sense of a use of language that runs (drivels?) on and on. *Courcourant* is derived from the neologism Lacan provided two paragraphs back, *disque-ourcourant*, by lopping off the "dis."
[32] *Bouchon*, which I have translated here as "cork," can also mean "stopper" or "plug"; it seems to put a stop here to this form of jouissance.
[33] Or "this jouissance, which she has owing to the fact of not being whole . . ." or "due to her not being whole . . ."

it with a true writing *(écrit),* insofar as the written is that aspect of language that is conditioned by a discourse.

4

The letter is, radically speaking, an effect of discourse.

What is nice about what I tell you – don't you agree? – is that it's always the same thing. Not that I repeat myself, that's not the point. It's that what I said before takes on meaning afterward.

The first time, as far as I recall, that I spoke of the letter – it must have been some fifteen years ago, somewhere at Sainte-Anne (Hospital) – I mentioned a fact known to everyone who reads a little, which is not the case for everyone, that a certain Sir Flinders Petrie believed he had discovered that the letters of the Phoenician alphabet existed well before the time of Phoenicia on small Egyptian pottery where they served as manufacturers' marks. That means that the letter first emerged from the market, which is typically an effect of discourse, before anyone dreamt of using letters to do what? Something that has nothing to do with the connotation of the signifier, but that elaborates and perfects it.

We should approach things at the level of the history of each language. It is clear that the letters which upset us so much that we call them, God only knows why, by a different name, "characters," to wit, Chinese letters, emerged from very ancient Chinese discourse in a way that was very different from the way in which our letters emerged. Emerging from analytic discourse, the letters I bring out here have a different value from those that can emerge from set theory. The uses one makes of them differ, but nevertheless – and this is what is of interest – they are not without converging in some respect. Any effect of discourse is good in the sense that it is constituted by the letter.

All of that is but a first sketch that I will have the opportunity to develop by distinguishing the use of letters in algebra from the use of letters in set theory. For the time being, I would simply like to point out the following – the world, the world is in [a state of] decomposition, thank God. We see that the world no longer stands up, because even in scientific discourse it is clear that there isn't the slightest world. As soon as you can add something called a "quark" to atoms and have that become the true thread of scientific discourse, you must realize that we are dealing with something other than a world.

You must sit down and read a little work by writers, not of your era – I won't tell you to read Philippe Sollers, who is unreadable, like me as a matter of fact – but you could read Joyce, for example. You will see therein how language is perfected when it knows how to play with writing.

I can agree that Joyce's work is not readable – it is certainly not translatable into Chinese. What happens in Joyce's work? The signifier stuffs *(vient truffer)*[34] the signified. It is because the signifiers fit together, combine, and concertina – read *Finnegans Wake* – that something is produced by way of meaning *(comme signifié)* that may seem enigmatic, but is clearly what is closest to what we analysts, thanks to analytic discourse, have to read – slips of the tongue *(lapsus)*.[35] It is as slips that they signify something, in other words, that they can be read in an infinite number of different ways. But it is precisely for that reason that they are difficult to read, are read awry, or not read at all. But doesn't this dimension of "being read" *(se lire)* suffice to show that we are in the register of analytic discourse?

What is at stake in analytic discourse is always the following – you give a different reading to the signifiers that are enunciated *(ce qui s'énonce de signifiant)* than what they signify.[36]

To make myself understood, I will take a reference you read in the great book of the world. Consider the flight of a bee. A bee goes from flower to flower gathering nectar. What you discover is that, at the tip of its feet, the bee transports pollen from one flower onto the pistil of another flower. That is what you read in the flight of the bee. In the flight of a bird that flies close to the ground – you call that a flight, but in reality it is a group at a certain level – you read that there is going to be a storm. But do they read? Does the bee read that it serves a function in the reproduction of phanerogamic plants? Does the bird read the portent of fortune, as people used to say – in other words, the tempest?

That is the whole question. It cannot be ruled out, after all, that a swallow reads the tempest, but it is not terribly certain either.

In your analytic discourse, you assume that the subject of the unconscious knows how to read. And this business of the unconscious is nothing other than that. Not only do you assume that it knows how to read, but you assume that it can learn how to read.

The only problem is that what you teach it to read has absolutely nothing to do, in any case, with what you can write of it.

January 9, 1973

[34] *Truffer* literally means to garnish with truffles; figuratively it means to stuff, lard, fill, or pepper.
[35] *Lapsus* is the usual French term for the broad Freudian category, "parapraxis," including slips of the tongue and of the pen, forgetting, and so on.
[36] Lacan's complicated phraseology would have us translate: "you give a different reading to what is enunciated qua signifier than what it signifies."

IV

Love and the signifier

THE OTHER SEX.[1]

CONTINGENCY OF THE SIGNIFIER, ROUTINE OF THE SIGNIFIED.

THE END OF THE WORLD AND THE "PARA-BEING."

LOVE MAKES UP FOR THE ABSENCE OF THE SEXUAL RELATIONSHIP.

THE ONES.

What can I still *(encore)* have to say to you after all the time this has lasted, without having all the effects that I would like? Well, it is precisely because it doesn't that I never run out of things to say.

Nevertheless, since one cannot say it all,[2] and for good reason, I am reduced to this narrow course, which is such that at every moment I must be careful not to slip back into what has already been done on the basis of what has been said.

That is why today I am going to try, once again, to stay this difficult ground-breaking course, whose horizon is strange, qualified, as it is, by my title – *Encore.*

1

The first time I spoke to you, I stated that jouissance of the Other – the Other I said to be symbolized by the body – is not a sign of love.[3]

Naturally, that goes over well, because you feel that it is at the same level as what I've said before *(le précédent dire)* and does not deviate therefrom.

Nevertheless, certain terms contained therein warrant commentary. Jouissance is exactly what I try to make present through this very act of speaking *(par ce dire même)*. "The Other" here is more than ever thrown into question.

On the one hand, the Other must be newly hammered out or recast for it to take on its full meaning, its complete resonance. On the other hand, it

[1] *L'Autre sexe* would normally be translated into English as "the opposite sex"; here, however, due to the capital *O*, I have translated it as "the Other sex." It should be kept in mind, nevertheless, that Lacan is playing off the two different meanings.
[2] *Tout dire* also means to "say everything."
[3] The exact quote from Chapter I is: "Jouissance of the Other, . . . , of the body of the Other who symbolizes the Other, is not the sign of love."

is important to put it forward as a term that is based on the fact that it is me who is speaking, and who can speak only from where I am, identified with a pure signifier. Man and a woman, as I said last time, are nothing but signifiers. They derive their function from this, from saying *(dire)* as a distinct incarnation of sex.

The Other, in my terminology, can thus only be the Other sex.   40

What is the status of this Other? What is its position with respect to this return on the basis of which *(de quoi)*[4] the sexual relationship is realized, namely, a jouissance, that analytic discourse has precipitated out as the function of the phallus, whose enigma remains utter and complete, since that function is articulated therein only on the basis of facts of absence?

But is that to say that what is at stake here is, as people all too quickly thought they could translate it, the signifier of what is lacking in the signifier? That is what this year ought to put an end to, and it should say what the function of the phallus is in analytic discourse. For the time being, I will say that what I put forward last time as the function of the bar is not unrelated to the phallus.

There is still the second part of the sentence linked to the first part by an "is not" – "is not the sign of love." And this year I shall have to articulate what serves as the linchpin of everything that has been instituted on the basis of analytic experience: love.

People have been talking about nothing else for a long time. Need I emphasize the fact that it is at the very heart of philosophical discourse? That is precisely what should make us suspicious. Last time, I had you catch a glimpse of philosophical discourse in its true light – as a variation on the master's discourse. I also said that love aims at being, namely, at what slips away most in language – being that, a moment later, was going to be,[5] or being that, due precisely to having been, gave rise to surprise. And I was also able to add that that being is perhaps very close to the signifier *m'être*,[6] is perhaps being at the helm *(l'être au commandement)*,[7] and that therein lies the strangest of illusions *(leurres)*. Doesn't that also command us to question in what sense the sign can be distinguished from the signifier?

Hence we have four points – jouissance, the Other, the sign, and love.

---

[4] The French, *de quoi* (which I have translated here as "on the basis of which"), is quite vague and could be translated in a number of other ways, including "in relation to which," "from which," "by which," etc.

[5] *Allait être* (was going to be) could also be translated as "would have been."

[6] The French allows us to read either "the signifier *m'être*" or "the *m'être* signifier," *m'être* being a homonym of *maître*, master (thus, "the master signifier").

[7] In a race, the person winning is said *d'être au commandement*, that is, to be "leading," "out in front," "heading the pack," or "first." However, in the last chapter, Lacan was more clearly referring to being at someone's orders.

Let us read what was put forward at a time when the discourse of love was admittedly that of being – let us open Richard of Saint Victor's book on the divine trinity.[8] We begin with being, being insofar as it is conceived – excuse me for slipping writing *(l'écrit)* into my speech – as "be-ternal-ing" *(l'êtrernel)*,[9] following Aristotle's elaboration, which is still so moderate, and under the influence, no doubt, of the eruption of the "I am what I am," which is the statement of Judaic truth.

When the idea of being – up until then simply approached or glancingly touched on – culminates in this violent ripping away from the function of time by the statement of the eternal, strange consequences ensue. There is, says Richard of Saint Victor, being that is intrinsically eternal,[10] being that is eternal but not intrinsically so, and being that is not eternal and does not possess its fragile or even inexistent being intrinsically. But there is no such thing as non-eternal being that is intrinsically. Of the four subdivisions that are produced by the alternation of affirmation and negation of "eternal" and "intrinsically," that is the only one that seems to Richard of Saint Victor to have to be ruled out.

41   Doesn't that have to do with the signifier? For no signifier is produced *(se produit)* as eternal.

That is no doubt what, rather than qualifying it as arbitrary, Saussure could have formulated – it would have been better to qualify the signifier with the category of contingency. The signifier repudiates the category of the eternal and, nevertheless, oddly enough *(singulièrement)*, it is intrinsically.

Isn't it clear to you that it participates, to employ a Platonic approach, in that nothing on the basis of which something entirely original was made *ex nihilo*, as creationism *(l'idée créationiste)* tells us?

---

[8] Book III of *The Trinity* can be found in English in *Richard of St. Victor: The Twelve Patriarchs, The Mystical Ark, and Book Three of the Trinity*, translated by Grover A. Zinn (New York: Paulist Press, 1979). Complete editions can be found in French: *La Trinité*, translated by Gaston Salet (Paris: Sources Chrétiennes, 1969), and *De Trinitate: texte critique*, translated by Jean Ribaillier (Paris: 1958).

[9] *L'êtrernel* is a conflation of *être* (being) and *éternel* (eternal), and perhaps of *lettre* (letter) as well. *L'Éternel* is a term for God.

[10] The expression I am rendering as "intrinsically" is *de lui-même*, literally "by itself" or "from itself" (as opposed to "because of someone or something else"). In certain contexts, it can take on the sense of "self-generated," "self-caused," or "self-based," and seems quite clearly to refer back to Aristotle's καθ' αὐτό. Terence Irwin and Gail Fine, in their translation of Aristotle's *Physics* (254b12–30) in *Aristotle: Selections* (Indianapolis: Hackett, 1995), provide the locution "by its own agency." Other possible translations include "in its own right," "in itself," "essentially" (as opposed to "coincidentally"), and "that by virtue of which." See Aristotle's extensive discussion of the term in *Metaphysics*, Book V, Chapter 18 (1022a14–36). Grover A. Zinn, in his translation of Book III of *The Trinity*, renders it simply as "from himself" (p. 373).

Isn't that something that appears *(apparaisse)* – insofar as your laziness *(laparesse)* can be shaken up by any sort of apparition – in the book of *Genesis? Genesis* recounts nothing other than the creation, from nothing, in effect – of what? – of nothing but signifiers.

As soon as this creation emerges, it is articulated on the basis of the naming of what is. Isn't that creation in its essence? While Aristotle cannot help but enunciate that, if ever there was anything, it had always been there, isn't what is at stake in creationism a creation on the basis of nothing – thus on the basis of the signifier?

Isn't that what we find in that which, being reflected in a world view, was enunciated as the Copernican revolution?

2

I have been throwing in doubt for a long time what Freud thought he could say about the said revolution. The hysteric's discourse taught him about that other substance, which consists entirely in the fact that there are signifiers *(il y a du signifiant)*. Having apprehended the effect of the signifier in the hysteric's discourse, he managed to turn the latter by the quarter turn that made it into analytic discourse.[11]

The very notion of a quarter turn evokes revolution, but certainly not in the sense in which revolution is subversion. On the contrary, what turns – that is what is called revolution – is destined, by its very statement *(énoncé),* to evoke a return.

Assuredly, we have by no means reached the completion of this return, since this quarter turn is being made in a very painful way. But it would not be an exaggeration to say that if there was, indeed, a revolution somewhere, it was certainly not at the level of Copernicus. The hypothesis had been advanced for many years that the sun was perhaps the center around which things revolved. But so what? What was of import to mathematicians was certainly the point of origin of that which turns. According to Aristotle, the eternal circling *(virée)*[12] of the stars in the last of the spheres presupposed an unmoved sphere, which was the first cause of the movement of those that revolve. If the stars revolve, it is because the earth itself turns. It was already wondrous that, on the basis of this circling, revolution, or eternal turning of the stellar sphere, there were men who forged other spheres, conceiving the so-called Ptolemaic system, and made the planets revolve –

42

---

[11] See Chapter II, section 1, where analytic discourse can be seen to result from the hysteric's discourse if each of the elements is rotated ninety degrees to the right.

[12] *Virée* generally means "swerve," "curve," or "veering."

planets that, with respect to the earth, are in the ambiguous position of coming and going in a zigzag pattern – revolve in accordance with an oscillatory movement.

Wasn't it an extraordinary tour de force to have conceptualized the movement of the spheres? Copernicus merely added the remark that perhaps the movement of the intermediary spheres could be expressed differently. Whether or not the earth lay at the center was not what was most important to him.

The Copernican revolution is by no means a revolution. If the center of a sphere is assumed, in a discourse that is merely analogical, to constitute the pivotal point *(point-maître)*, the fact of changing this pivotal point, of having it be occupied by the earth or the sun, involves nothing that in itself subverts what the signifier "center" intrinsically *(de lui-même)* preserves. Man – what is designated by this term, which is nothing but that which makes (things) signify – was far from ever having been shaken by the discovery that the earth is not at the center. He had no problem substituting the sun for it.

Of course it is now obvious that the sun is not a center either, and that it is strolling through a space whose status is ever more precariously established. What remains at the center is the fine routine that is such that the signified always retains the same meaning *(sens)* in the final analysis. That meaning is provided by the sense each of us has of being part of his world, that is, of his little family and of everything that revolves around it. Each of you – I am speaking even for the leftists – you are more attached to it than you care to know and would do well to sound the depths of your attachment. A certain number of biases are your daily fare and limit the import of your insurrections to the shortest term, to the term, quite precisely, that gives you no discomfort – they certainly don't change your world view, for that remains perfectly spherical. The signified finds its center wherever you take it. And, unless things change radically, it is not analytic discourse – which is so difficult to sustain in its decentering and has not yet made its entrance into common consciousness – that can in any way subvert anything whatsoever.

Nevertheless, if you will allow me to make use of this Copernican reference, I will stress what is effective about it. It's not the fact of changing the center.

It turns. That fact still has a great deal of value for us, as reduced as it may be in the final analysis, motivated only by the fact that the earth turns and that it therefore seems to us that it is the celestial sphere that turns. The earth continues to turn and that has all sorts of effects, for example, the fact that you count your age in years. The subversion, if it existed some-

where, at some time, was not that of having changed the point around 43
which it circles *(point de virée)* – it is that of having replaced "it turns" with
"it falls."

What is crucial, as some people have noticed, is not Copernicus, but
more specifically Kepler, due to the fact that in his work it does not turn in
the same way – it turns in an ellipse, and that already throws into question
the function of the center. That toward which it falls in Kepler's work is a
point of the ellipse that is called a focus, and in the symmetrical point there
is nothing. That is assuredly a corrective to the image of the center. But "it
falls" only takes on the weight of subversion when it leads to what? To this
and nothing more:

$$F = g\frac{mm'}{d^2}.$$

It is in this writing *(écrit)*, in what is summarized in these five little letters
that can be written in the palm of your hand, and one number to boot, that
consists what we unduly attribute to Copernicus. This is what rips us away
from the imaginary function – nevertheless grounded in the real – of revolution.

What is produced in the articulation of the new discourse that emerges
as analytic discourse is that the function of the signifier is taken as the starting point, for what the signifier brings with it by way of meaning effects is
far from accepted on the basis of the lived experience of the very fact.

It is on the basis of meaning effects that the structuring of which I
reminded you was constructed. For quite some time it seemed natural for
a world to be constituted whose correlate, beyond it, was being itself, being
taken as eternal. This world conceived of as the whole *(tout)*, with what this
word implies by way of limitation, regardless of the openness we grant it,
remains a conception[13] – a serendipitous term here – a view, gaze, or imaginary hold. And from that results the following, which remains strange, that
some-one – a part of this world – is at the outset assumed to be able to take
cognizance of it. This One finds itself therein in a state that we can call
existence, for how could it be the basis of the "taking cognizance" if it did
not exist? Therein has always lain the impasse, the vacillation resulting from
the cosmology that consists in the belief in a world. On the contrary, isn't
there something in analytic discourse that can introduce us to the following:
that every subsistence or persistence of the world as such must be aban-
doned?

[13] Thus far, I have been translating *conception du monde* as "world view"; here
conception appears alone. *Conception* has the same double meaning in French as in
English: "view (or notion)" and "inception of pregnancy."

Language – the language *(langue)* forged by philosophical discourse – is such that, as you see, I cannot but constantly slip back into this world, into this presupposition of a substance that is permeated[14] with the function of being.

3

Following the thread of analytic discourse goes in the direction of nothing less than breaking up anew *(rebriser)*, inflecting, marking with its own camber – a camber that could not even be sustained as that of lines of force – that which produces the break *(faille)* or discontinuity. Our recourse, in llanguage *(lalangue)*,[15] is to that which shatters it *(la brise)*.[16] Hence nothing seems to better constitute the horizon of analytic discourse than the use made of the letter by mathematics. The letter reveals in discourse what is called – not by chance or without necessity – grammar. Grammar is that aspect of language that is revealed only in writing *(à l'écrit)*.

Beyond language, this effect, which is produced by being based only on writing, is certainly the ideal of mathematics. Now to refuse to refer to writing *(l'écrit)* is to forbid oneself what can actually be articulated using *(de)* all the effects of language. This articulation occurs in what results from language regardless of what we do – namely, a presumed shy of and beyond *(en deçà et au-delà)*.

We certainly sense that this shy of is no more than an intuitive reference. And yet this presupposition cannot be eliminated because language, in its meaning effect, is never but beside the referent.[17] Isn't it thus true that language imposes being upon us and obliges us, as such, to admit that we never have anything by way of being *(de l'être)*?

What we must get used to is substituting the "para-being" *(par-être)* – the being *"para,"* being beside – for the being that would take flight.[18]

I say the "para-being" *(par-être)*, and not the "appearing" *(paraître)*,[19]

---

[14] The term Lacan uses here, *imprégnée*, also means "impregnated," but primarily in the sense of saturated, not of fertilization.

[15] The French here, *lalangue*, is a term Lacan creates simply by putting together the feminine article *la* with the noun *langue* (language, but specifically spoken language, as in tongue). Lacan discusses what he means by *lalangue* in the course of this Seminar (as well as elsewhere); very roughly speaking, it has to do with the acoustic level of language, the level at which polysemy is possible due to the existence of homonyms (like those Lacan plays on throughout this Seminar). It is the level at which an infant (or songwriter) may endlessly repeat one syllable of a word (for example, "la la la"), the level at which language may "stutter" – hence the translation provided here, borrowed from Russell Grigg, "llanguage."

[16] *La* here could refer to "break," "discontinuity," or "llanguage."

[17] The French here, *à côté du référent*, could also be translated as "alongside the referent."

[18] *Fuir* (to take flight) also means "to leak."

[19] The neologism Lacan creates here, *par-être*, is pronounced exactly like *paraître*, which means "to appear" or "appearing." Two sentences further on, Lacan

as the phenomenon has always been called – that beyond which there is supposedly that thing, the noumenon. The latter has, in effect, led us, led us to all sorts of opacifications[20] that can be referred to precisely as obscurantism. It is at the very point at which paradoxes spring up regarding everything that manages to be formulated as the effect of writing *(effet d'écrit)* that being presents itself, always presents itself, by para-being.[21] We should learn to conjugate that appropriately: I par-am, you par-are, he par-is, we par-are, and so on and so forth.

It is in relation to the para-being that we must articulate what makes up for *(supplée au)*[22] the sexual relationship qua nonexistent. It is clear that, in everything that approaches it, language merely manifests its inadequacy.

What makes up for the sexual relationship is, quite precisely, love.

The Other, the Other as the locus of truth, is the only place, albeit an irreducible place, that we can give to the term "divine being," God, to call him by his name. God *(Dieu)* is the locus where, if you will allow me this wordplay, the *dieu* – the *dieur* – the *dire*, is produced. With a trifling change, the *dire* constitutes *Dieu.*[23] And as long as things are said, the God hypothesis will persist.

That is why, in the end, only theologians can be truly atheistic, namely, those who speak of God.

There is no other way to be an atheist, except to hide one's head in one's arms in the name of I know not what fear, as if this God had ever manifested any kind of presence whatsoever. Nevertheless, it is impossible to say anything without immediately making Him subsist in the form of the Other.

That is quite evident in even the slightest movement of something I can't stand, for the best of reasons, that is, History.

People do History precisely in order to make us believe that it has some

intends both meanings when he says that "being presents itself, always presents itself, by *par-être*," i.e., by appearing and being beside (or alongside).
[20] The French, *opacification,* is originally a medical term for the decrease in transparency of the cornea or crystalline lens. Lacan plays in this sentence on the similar French pronunciation of *noumène* ("noumenon") and *nous mène* ("leads us").
[21] *Par-être* could also be rendered by the neologistic "ap-bc-aring beside" or "appbesiding."
[22] The French, *supplée au rapport sexuel,* could more literally be translated as "supplements the sexual relationship." The end of the next sentence could be more literally translated as "language manifests itself merely in (or on the basis of) its inadequacy."
[23] The French, *Pour un rien, le dire ça fait Dieu,* is far more polysemic than my translation here; by translating it as "For a nothing, the saying amounts to God," one can see speech's godlike power to create *ex nihilo. Fait* here can be either "creates" or "plays the part of," "turns into" or "becomes." *Dieur,* in the last sentence, is a neologism, but since it is constructed like many other French terms, it can literally be understood to mean "sayer" or "speaker" (thus, the speaking god or the speaker as god).

sort of meaning. On the contrary, the first thing we must do is begin from the following: we are confronted with a saying *(dire)*, the saying *(dire)* of another person who recounts his stupidities, embarrassments, inhibitions, and emotions *(émois)*.[24] What is it that we must read therein? Nothing but the effects of those instances of saying *(dires)*. We see in what sense these effects agitate, stir things up, and bother speaking beings. Of course, for that to lead to something, it must serve them, and it does serve them, by God, in working things out, accommodating themselves, and managing all the same – in a bumbling, stumbling sort of way – to give a shadow of life to the feeling known as love.

It must, it really must, it must last longer *(encore)*. It must, with the help of this feeling, lead, in the end – as people have seen who, with respect to all of this, have taken their precautions under the aegis of the Church – to the reproduction of bodies.

But isn't it possible that language may have other effects than to lead people by the nose to reproduce yet again *(encore)*, in the body to body *(en corps à corps)*,[25] and in incarnated bodies *(en corps incarné)*?

There is another effect of language, which is writing *(l'écrit)*.

4

We have seen changes in writing *(l'écrit)* since language has existed. What is written are letters, and letters have not always been fabricated in the same way. On that subject, people do history, the history of writing, and people rack their brains imagining what purpose the Mayan and Aztec pictographs might have served and, a bit further back in time, the pebbles of the Mas d'Azil[26] – what could those funny sort of dice have been, and what kind of games did they play with them?

To raise such questions is the habitual function of History. One should say – above all, don't touch that H,[27] the initial of History. That would be a fine way of bringing people back to the first of the letters, the one to which I confine my attention, the letter A. The Bible begins, by the way, only with the letter B – it left behind the letter A so that I could take charge of it.

There is a lot to learn here, not by studying the pebbles of the Mas d'Azil,

---

24 On the distinctions Lacan draws between *embarras*, *empêchement*, and *émoi*, see Seminar X, *Anxiety*.

25 In French, *en corps* is pronounced exactly like *encore*. *Corps à corps* is usually translated as "hand to hand" (combat, for example).

26 The Mas d'Azil is an area in southern France where artifacts from the Azilian industry, a tool tradition of Late Paleolithic and Early Mesolithic Europe, have been found. Art seems to have been confined to geometric drawings made on pebbles using red and black pigments.

27 The letter *H* is pronounced exactly like *hache* in French, which means "ax" or "hatchet."

nor even, as I formerly did for my receptive audience *(bon public)*,[28] my receptive audience of analysts, by seeking out the notch on the stone to explain the unary trait[29] – that was within their ken – but by looking more closely at what mathematicians have been doing with letters since, scorning a number of things, they began, in the most well grounded of fashions, under the name of set theory, to notice that one could approach the One in a way other than the intuitive, fusional, amorous way.

"We are but one." Everyone knows, of course, that two have never become but one, but nevertheless "we are but one." The idea of love begins with that. It is truly the crudest way of providing the sexual relationship, that term that manifestly slips away, with its signified.

The beginning of wisdom should involve beginning to realize that it is in that respect that old father Freud broke new ground. I myself began with that because it affected me quite a bit myself. It could affect anyone, moreover, couldn't it, to realize that love, while it is true that it has a relationship with the One, never makes anyone leave himself behind.[30] If that, all of that and nothing but that, is what Freud said by introducing the function of narcissistic love, everyone senses and sensed that the problem is how there can be love for an other.

The One everyone talks about all the time is, first of all, a kind of mirage of the One you believe yourself to be. Not to say that that is the whole horizon. There are as many Ones as you like – they are characterized by the fact that none of them resemble any of the others in any way – see the first hypothesis in the *Parmenides*.

Set theory bursts onto the scene by positing the following: let us speak of things as One that are strictly unrelated to each other. Let us put together objects of thought, as they are called, objects of the world, each of which counts as one. Let us assemble these absolutely heterogeneous things, and let us grant ourselves the right to designate the resulting assemblage by a letter. That is how set theory expresses itself at the outset, that theory, for example, that I mentioned last time in relation to Nicolas Bourbaki.

You let slip by the fact that I said that the letter designates an assemblage. That is what is printed in the text of the definitive edition to which the authors – as you know, there are several of them – ended up consenting. They are very careful to say that letters designate assemblages. Therein lies their timidity and their error – letters *constitute (font)*[31] assemblages. They

---

[28] While *bon public* literally means "good audience," it also implies that they are receptive to or appreciate whatever Lacan says (no matter how absurd).

[29] See Seminar IX, *Identification*.

[30] *Sortir quiconque de soi-même* could also be translated as "go beyond himself."

[31] *Font* here can also mean "create" or "play the part of."

don't *designate* assemblages, they *are* assemblages. They are taken as *(comme)* functioning like *(comme)* these assemblages themselves.

You see that by still preserving this "like" *(comme)*, I am staying within the bounds of what I put forward when I say that the unconscious is structured *like* a language. I say *like* so as not to say – and I come back to this all the time – that the unconscious is structured *by* a language. The unconscious is structured like the assemblages in question in set theory, which are like letters.[32]

Since what is at stake for us is to take language as *(comme)* that which functions in order to make up for the absence of the sole part of the real that cannot manage to be formed from being *(se former de l'être)* – namely, the sexual relationship – what basis can we find in merely reading letters? It is in the very play of mathematical writing *(l'écrit)* that we must find the compass reading toward which to head in order to draw from this practice – from this new social link, analytic discourse, that emerges and spreads in such a singular fashion – what can be drawn from it regarding the function of language, that language in which we put our faith in order for this discourse to have effects – middling, no doubt, but tolerable enough – so that this discourse can prop up and complete the other discourses.

For some time now, it has been clear that university discourse must be written "uni-vers-Cythera,"[33] since it must teach sex education. We shall see what that will lead to. We certainly shouldn't try to block it. The idea that something may be imparted regarding this bit *(point)* of knowledge – which is placed *(se pose)* exactly in the authoritarian situation of semblance – that can improve relations between the sexes is certainly destined to bring a smile to an analyst's face. But after all, who knows?

As I already said, the angel's smile is the stupidest of smiles, and one must thus never brag about it. But it is clear that the very idea of demonstrating something related to sex education on the blackboard does not seem, from the vantage point of the analyst's discourse, to promise much in the way of fortunate encounters or happiness.

If there is something in my *Écrits* that shows that my fine orientation, since it is of that fine orientation that I try to convince you, is not such a recent development, it is the fact that right after a war, where nothing obviously seemed to promise a pretty future, I wrote "Logical Time and the Assertion of Anticipated Certainty."[34] One can quite easily read therein – if

---

[32] There is a problem here in the French text; given the context, I have assumed that the word *qui* should be inserted between *ensembles* and *sont* (in *L'inconscient est structuré comme les assemblages dont il s'agit dans la théorie des ensembles sont comme les lettres*).

[33] Cythera (or Kithira) is the southernmost of the Ionian Islands in Greece, and is reputed to be the island of Aphrodite, an island of love and pleasure.

[34] Translated into English by Bruce Fink and Marc Silver, in *Newsletter of the Freudian Field* 2 (1988), pp. 4–22.

one writes and not only if one has a good ear – that it is already little *a* that thetisizes the function of haste. In that article, I highlighted the fact that something like intersubjectivity can lead to a salutary solution *(issue)*. But what warrants a closer look is what each of the subjects sustains *(supporte),* not insofar as he is one among others, but insofar as he is, in relation to the two others, what is at stake in their thinking. Each intervenes in this ternary only as the object *a* that he is in the gaze of the others.

In other words, there are three of them, but in reality, there are two plus *a*. This two plus *a*, from the standpoint of *a*, can be reduced, not to the two others, but to a One plus *a*. You know, moreover, that I have already used these functions to try to represent to you the inadequacy of the relationship between the One and the Other, and that I have already provided as a basis for this little *a* the irrational number known as the golden number.[35] It is insofar as, starting from little *a*,[36] the two others are taken as One plus *a*, that what can lead to an exit in haste functions.

48

This identification, which is produced in a ternary articulation, is grounded in the fact that in no case can two as such serve as a basis. Between two, whatever they may be, there is always the One and the Other, the One and the *a,* and the Other cannot in any way be taken as a One.

It is insofar as something brutal is played out in writing *(l'écrit)* – namely, the taking as ones of as many ones as we like – that the impasses that are revealed thereby are, by themselves, a possible means of access to being for us and a possible reduction of the function of that being in love.

I want to end by showing in what respect the sign can be distinguished from the signifier.

The signifier, as I have said, is characterized by the fact that it represents a subject to another signifier. What is involved in the sign? The cosmic theory of knowledge or world view has always made a big deal of the famous example of smoke that cannot exist without fire.[37] So why shouldn't I put forward what I think about it? Smoke can just as easily be the sign of a smoker. And, in essence, it always is. There is no smoke that is not a sign of a smoker. Everyone knows that, if you see smoke when you approach a deserted island, you immediately say to yourself that there is a good chance there is someone there who knows how to make fire. Until things change considerably, it will be another man. Thus, a sign is not the sign of some thing, but of an effect that is what is presumed as such by a functioning of the signifier.

[35] On the golden number, see, in particular, Seminar XIV, *The Logic of Fantasy,* and Seminar XVI, *From one Other to the other.*

[36] The French, *du petit a,* could mean "from the standpoint of little *a,*" "on the basis of little *a,*" and other things as well.

[37] Lacan is referring here to the proverb, *il n'y a pas de fumée sans feu,* "there's no smoke without fire."

That effect is what Freud teaches us about, and it is the starting point of analytic discourse, namely, the subject.

The subject is nothing other than what slides in a chain of signifiers, whether he knows which signifier he is the effect of or not. That effect – the subject – is the intermediary effect between what characterizes a signifier and another signifier, namely, the fact that each of them, each of them is an element. We know of no other basis by which the One may have been introduced into the world if not by the signifier as such, that is, the signifier insofar as we learn to separate it from its meaning effects.

In love what is aimed at is the subject, the subject as such, insofar as he is presumed in an articulated sentence, in something that is organized or can be organized on the basis of a whole life.

A subject, as such, doesn't have much to do with jouissance. But, on the other hand, his sign is capable of arousing desire. Therein lies the mainspring of love. The course I will try to continue to steer in our next classes will show you where love and sexual jouissance meet up.

January 16, 1973

Aristotle and Freud:
the other satisfaction

"All the needs of speaking beings are contaminated by the fact of being involved in an other satisfaction" – underline the last three words – "that those needs may not live up to."[1]

This first sentence, which I wrote down this morning when I woke up so that you would write it down, sweeps away the opposition between an other satisfaction and needs – assuming this term ["needs"], which people so often resort to, can be so easily grasped, since, after all, it can only be grasped by not living up to *(faire défaut à)* that other satisfaction.

The other satisfaction is, as you must realize,[2] what is satisfied at the level of the unconscious – insofar as something is said there and is not said there, if it is true that it is structured like a language.

Here I am coming back to something I have been referring to for some time, namely, the jouissance on which that other satisfaction depends, the one[3] that is based on language.

1

In dealing, a long time ago, a very long time ago indeed, with the ethics of psychoanalysis, I began with nothing less than Aristotle's *Nicomachean Ethics.*

That can be read. There is only one problem for a certain number of you here, and that is that it cannot be read in French. It is manifestly untranslat-

---

[1] Lacan's French here, *à quoi ils peuvent faire défaut*, is quite ambiguous; it could suggest that those needs may come up short as regards that other satisfaction, not live up to it, or default on it.

[2] The French here, *vous devez l'entendre*, suggests that Lacan expects us to hear, realize, or grasp what is to follow in the sentence from the very expression "the other satisfaction" (and perhaps from the general theme of the Seminar thus far).

[3] Lacan does not repeat the noun, jouissance, here. Instead he simply says *celle* ("the one"), which could refer either to jouissance or the other satisfaction.

able. A long time ago, the Garnier publishing company came out with something that might have made me believe there was a translation, by someone named Voilquin. He was an academic, obviously. It's not his fault if Greek cannot be translated into French. Things have gotten condensed in such a way that Garnier, which, moreover, has since merged with Flammarion, no longer gives you anything but the French text – I must say that publishers infuriate me. You all notice then, when you read it without the Greek on opposite pages, that you can't make head nor tail of it. It is, strictly speaking, unintelligible.

"All art and all research, like all action and all reflected deliberation" – what relation could there possibly be among those four things? – "tend, it seems, toward some good. Thus people have sometimes had good reason to define the good as that towards which one tends in all circumstances. Nevertheless" – and this comes out of the blue, not having yet been discussed – "it seems that there is a difference between ends."[4]

I challenge anyone to be able to clear away this thick morass without abundant commentary referring to the Greek text. It seems quite impossible that the text could sound like this simply because we have but badly taken notes. After a while, a light bulb flashes on in the heads of certain commentators – it dawns on them that, if they are obliged to work so hard, maybe there's a reason for it. Aristotle need not be unthinkable at all – I'll come back to this point.

In my own case, what wound up being written – that is, typed up on the basis of the stenography[5] – concerning what I had said about ethics seemed more than utilizable by the people who were, nevertheless, simultaneously engaged in pointing me out to the attention of the *Internationale de psychanalyse*[6] with the result that is well known. They would have liked to see preserved, all the same, my reflections on what psychoanalysis brings with it by way of ethics. It would have been sheer profit [for them] – I would have sunk to the bottom while *The Ethics of Psychoanalysis* would have stayed afloat. That's an example of the fact that calculation is not enough –

---

[4] The passage of which Lacan is quoting the French translation is the very first paragraph of the *Nicomachean Ethics* (1094a); here is the text of a very recent English translation of the passage: "Every craft and every investigation, and likewise every action and decision, seems to aim at some good; hence the good has been well described as that at which everything aims. However, there is an apparent difference among the ends aimed at" (*Aristotle: Selections*, translated by Terence Irwin and Gail Fine [Indianapolis: Hackett, 1995], p. 347).

[5] A stenographer began to transcribe Lacan's seminars starting in 1952. Lacan had, in fact, begun giving his seminar two years before that, but no stenographer was present and only a few notes taken by Lacan's students remain.

[6] Lacan seems to be deliberately distorting the name of the International Psychoanalytical Association (IPA), generally known in French as the *Association psychanalytique internationale;* Lacan's name for it evokes the communist Internationals. Lacan was essentially forced out of the IPA in 1963, three years after he gave Seminar VII, *The Ethics of Psychoanalysis* (1959–1960).

I stopped my *Ethics* from being published. I refused to allow it to come out because I'm not going to try to convince people who want nothing to do with me. One must not convince *(convaincre)*. What is proper to psycho-analysis is not to vanquish *(vaincre)*, regardless of whether people are ass-holes *(con)* or not.[7]

It wasn't at all a bad seminar, in the end. At the time, someone who did not in any way participate in the calculation I just mentioned, wrote it up as he could, making an honest, wholehearted effort. He made it into a writ-ten text, a written text by him. He hadn't even thought of stealing it from me, and he would have published it like that if I had been willing. But I wasn't. Today, of all the seminars that someone else is going to bring out, it is perhaps the only one I will rewrite myself and make into a written text. I really should do one, all the same. Why not pick that one?

There's no reason not to put oneself to the test, not to see how others before Freud saw the terrain in which he constituted his field. It is another way of experiencing what is involved, namely, that this terrain is unthink-able except with the help of the instruments with which we operate, and that the only instruments by which accounts are conveyed are writings. A very simple test makes this clear – reading the *Nicomachean Ethics* in the French translation, you understand nothing in it, of course, but no less than in what I tell you, and thus it suffices all the same.

Aristotle is no more comprehensible than what I talk to you about. It is even less comprehensible because he stirs up more things and things that are further from us. But it is clear that the other satisfaction I was talking about earlier is exactly the satisfaction that can be seen to emerge from what? Well, my good friends, there's no escaping it if you force yourself to look at it closely *(au pied du truc)*[8] – from the universals: the Good, Truth, and Beauty.

But the fact that there are these three specifications gives an air of pathos to the approach adopted by certain texts, those that are "authorized," with the meaning I give that term when placed in quotes, namely, those that are bequeathed to us under an author's name. That is what happens with cer-tain texts that come to us from what I think twice about calling a very ancient culture – it's not culture.

Culture, insofar as it is distinct from society, doesn't exist. Culture is the

---

[7] In the present context, *un con* means "an idiot," "an asshole," "a jerk," and so on; as an adjective, *con* means "stupid," "idiotic," etc. In playing on the words *vaincre* and *convaincre*, Lacan is saying that, in psychoanalysis, there is no point trying to win over or convince jerks.

[8] Lacan has modified here the usual French expression *être au pied du mur,* "to be up against it," or "with one's back to the wall," by saying *si vous vous mettez au pied du truc.* That implies, it seems to me, putting yourself up against it, but also evokes the expression, *prendre quelque chose au pied de la lettre,* "to take something literally."

51

fact that it has a hold on us *(ça nous tient)*. We no longer have it on our backs, except in the form of vermin, because we don't know what to do with it, except to get ourselves deloused. I recommend that you keep it, because it tickles and wakes you up. That will awaken your feelings that tend rather to become a bit deadened[9] under the influence of ambient conditions, in other words, due to what others who come afterward will call your culture. It will have become culture for them because you will have already been six feet under for a long time and, with you, everything that you sustain qua social link. In the final analysis, there's nothing but that, the social link. I designate it with the term "discourse" because there's no other way to designate it once we realize that the social link is instated only by anchoring itself in the way in which language is situated over and etched into what the place is crawling with, namely, speaking beings.

We shouldn't be astonished by the fact that former discourses – and there will be others to follow – are no longer thinkable to us or thinkable only with great difficulty. Just as the discourse I am trying to bring to light is not immediately accessible to your understanding, similarly, from where we stand, it is not very easy to understand Aristotle's discourse. But is that a reason why it should no longer be thinkable? It is quite clear that it is thinkable. It is only when we imagine that Aristotle means something that we worry about what he is encompassing. What is he catching in his net, in his network? What is he drawing out of it? What is he handling? What is he dealing with? What is he struggling with? What is he maintaining? What is he working on? What is he pursuing?

Obviously, in the first four lines [of Aristotle's *Ethics*] that I read to you, you hear words, and you assume they mean something, but naturally you don't know what. "All art, all research, all action" – what does all of that mean? It's because Aristotle threw in a lot of stuff after that, and because it comes down to us in printed form after having been copied and recopied for a long time, that we assume there must be something there that grabs one *(fait prise)*. That is when we raise the question, the only question – at what level did such things satisfy them?

It makes little difference what use was made of them at the time. We know that they were passed down and that there were volumes of Aristotle's work. That disconcerts us, and it does so precisely because the question "At what level did such things satisfy them?" is translatable only as follows: "At what level might a certain jouissance have been to blame?"[10] In other words, why – why did he get so worked up *(se tracassait)?*

[marginal: 52]

---

[9] The French term Lacan uses here, *abrutis,* can also be translated as "moronic" or "idiotic."
[10] The French term, *faute,* recalls the *faire défaut* used at the very beginning of this lecture, and can mean "sin," "fault," "error," and so on. In the expression

You heard me right – failing, deficiency *(faute, défaut)*,[11] something that isn't working out *(qui ne va pas)*. Something skids off track in what is manifestly aimed at, and then it immediately starts up with the good and happiness. The good, the bad, and the oafish! *(Du bi, du bien, du benêt!)*[12]

2

"Reality is approached with apparatuses of jouissance."[13]

That is another formulation I am proposing to you, as long as we focus, of course, on the fact that there's no other apparatus than language. That is how jouissance is fitted out *(appareillée)* in speaking beings.

That is what Freud says, assuming we correct the statement of the pleasure principle. He said it the way he did because there were others who had spoken before him, and that seemed to him the way it could most easily be heard. It is very easy to isolate, and the conjunction of Aristotle with Freud helps us isolate it.

I push further ahead, at the point at which it can now be done, by saying that the unconscious is structured like a language. On that basis, language is clarified, no doubt, by being posited as the apparatus of jouissance. But inversely, perhaps jouissance shows that in itself it is deficient *(en défaut)* – for, in order for it to be that way, something about it mustn't be working.

Reality is approached with apparatuses of jouissance. That doesn't mean that jouissance is prior to reality. Freud left the door open to misunderstanding on that score – you can find his discussion in what is known in French as the *Essais de Psychanalyse*.[14]

There is, says Freud, a *Lust-Ich* before a *Real-Ich*. That is tantamount to slipping back into the rut, the rut I call "development," which is merely a hypothesis of mastery. It suggests that a baby has nothing to do with the

---

faute à une certaine jouissance, it is that certain jouissance that is to blame, that has sinned, come up short, proved inadequate, deficient, lacking, failing, etc.

[11] See footnotes 1 and 10 above regarding these highly polyvalent French nouns.

[12] Lacan seems to be playing off a somewhat nonsensical French advertisement for a liquor called Dubonet, which was well known at the time: *"Du du, du bon, Dubonet";* he may also be intentionally mimicking the sounds of certain jazz vocals – dooby dooby do.

[13] The French here, *les appareils de la jouissance,* could also be translated as "jouissance devices."

[14] Lacan may be referring here to the footnote on page 135 of the French collection of Freud's work entitled *Essais de Psychanalyse* (Paris: Payot, 1981 [the earlier edition contained the same texts in an older translation]), where Freud talks about "the child's development into a mature adult" (SE XVIII, p. 79). Freud's references to the "pleasure-ego" and the "reality-ego" can be found, above all, in "Formulations on the Two Principles of Mental Functioning" (1911), "Instincts and their Vicissitudes" (1915), and "Negation" (1925).

Real-Ich, poor tot, and is incapable of having the slightest notion of the real. That is reserved for people we know, adults concerning whom, moreover, it is expressly stated that they never manage to wake up – when something happens in their dreams that threatens to cross over into the real, it distresses them so much that they immediately awaken, in other words, they go on dreaming. It suffices to read, be with them a little bit, see them live, and listen to them in analysis to realize what "development" means.

When we say "primary" and "secondary" for the processes, that may well be a manner of speaking that fosters an illusion. Let's say, in any case, that it is not because a process is said to be primary – we can call them whatever we want, after all – that it is the first to appear. Personally, I have never looked at a baby and had the sense that there was no outside world for him. It is plain to see that a baby looks at nothing but that, that it excites him, and that that is the case precisely to the extent that he does not yet speak. From the moment he begins to speak, from that exact moment onward and not before, I can understand that there is [such a thing as] repression. The process of the *Lust-Ich* may be primary – why not? it's obviously primary once we begin to think – but it's certainly not the first.

Development is confused with the development of mastery. It is here that one must have a good ear, like in music – I am the master *(m'être),* I progress along the path of mastery *(m'êtrise),* I am the master *(m'être)* of myself *(moi)* as I am of the universe. That is what I was talking about earlier, the vanquished idiot *(con-vaincu).* The universe is a flower of rhetoric. This literary echo may perhaps help us understand that the ego *(moi)* can also be a flower of rhetoric, which grows in the pot of the pleasure principle that Freud calls *"Lustprinzip,"* and that I define as that which is satisfied by blah-blah.

That is what I am saying when I say that the unconscious is structured like a language. But I must dot the i's and cross the t's. The universe – you might realize it by now, all the same, given the way in which I have accentuated the use of certain words, the "whole" and the "not-whole," and their differential application to the two sexes – the universe is the place where, due to the fact of speaking, everything succeeds *(de dire, tout réussit).*

Am I going to do a little William James here? Succeeds in what? I can tell you the answer, now that I have, I hope, finally managed to bring you to this point: succeeds in making the sexual relationship fail *(faire rater)*[15] in the male manner.

Normally I would expect to hear some snickering now – alas, I don't hear any. Snickering would mean "So, you've admitted it, there are two ways to

---

[15] *Rater* means to "fail," "botch," "screw up," "mess up," etc. I have translated it in a number of different ways in this chapter.

make the sexual relationship fail." That is how the music of the epithala-mion[16] is modulated. The epithalamion, the duet *(duo)* – one must distin-guish the two of them – the alternation, the love letter, they're not the sexual relationship. They revolve around the fact that there's no such thing as a sexual relationship.

There is thus the male way of revolving around it, and then the other one, that I will not designate otherwise because it's what I'm in the process of elaborating this year – how that is elaborated in the female way. It is 54 elaborated on the basis of the not-whole. But as, up until now, the not-whole has not been amply explored, it's obviously giving me a hard time.

On that note, I am going to tell you a good one to distract you a bit.

In the middle of my winter sports, I felt that I had to go to Milan by rail in order to keep my word. It took up a whole day just to get there. In short, I went to Milan, and as I cannot but talk about what I'm working on at the moment, that's the way I am – I said that I would rework *The Ethics of Psychoanalysis*, but that's because I'm drawing it out anew[17] – I picked an absolutely ridiculous title for my lecture to the Milanese, who had never heard anyone talk about such things before, "Psychoanalysis in Reference to the Sexual Relationship." They are very intelligent. They understood it so well that immediately, that very evening, the following was printed in the newspaper, "According to Dr. Lacan, Ladies" – *le donne* – "Do Not Exist!"

It's true – what do you expect? – if the sexual relationship doesn't exist, there aren't any ladies. There was someone who was furious, a lady from the women's liberation movement down there. She was truly. . . . I said to her, "Come tomorrow morning, and I'll explain to you what it's all about."

If there is some angle from which this business of the sexual relationship could be clarified, it's precisely from the ladies' side *(côté)*, insofar as it is on the basis of the elaboration of the not-whole that one must break new ground. That is my true subject this year, behind *Encore*, and it is one of the meanings of my title. Perhaps I will manage, in this way, to bring out something new regarding feminine sexuality.

There is one thing that provides dazzling evidence of this not-whole. Consider how, with one of these nuances or oscillations of signification that are produced in language *(langue)*, the not-whole changes meaning when I say to you, "Regarding feminine sexuality, our colleagues, the lady analysts, do *not* tell us . . . the *whole* story!" *(pas tout!)*. It's quite striking.[18] They

---

[16] A nuptial poem or song in honor of a bride and bridegroom.

[17] *Je la réextrais* literally means "I am re-extracting it, mining it, drawing it out (of the ground)."

[18] Unfortunately, the word play is *not* very striking in English; I have not found a way to work "not whole" into such a formulation directly, without the interposition of other words.

haven't contributed one iota to the question of feminine sexuality. There must be an internal reason for that, related to the structure of the apparatus of jouissance.

3

That brings me back to what I myself earlier raised by way of objections to myself, all by myself, namely, that there was a male way of botching *(rater)* the sexual relationship, and then another. This botching *(ratage)* is the only way of realizing that relationship if, as I posit, there's no such thing as a sexual relationship. To say, thus, that everything succeeds does not stop us from saying "not-everything succeeds" *(pas-tout réussit)*, for it is in the same manner – it fails *(ça rate)*. It's not a matter of analyzing how it succeeds. It's a matter of repeating until you're blue in the face why it fails.

It fails. That is objective. I have already stressed that. Indeed, it is so plain that it is objective that one must center the question of the object in analytic discourse thereupon. The failure is the object.

I already said long ago in what respect the good and the bad object differ. There is the good, there is the bad, oh la la! Today I am trying to begin with that, with what is related to what's good *(le bon)*, the good *(le bien)*, and to what Freud enunciates. The object is a failure *(un raté)*. The essence of the object is failure.

You will notice that I spoke of essence, just like Aristotle. So? That means that such old words are entirely usable. At a time when I dragged my feet less than today, that is what I turned to right after Aristotle. I said that, if something freshened the air a bit after all this Greek foot-dragging around Eudemonism,[19] it was certainly the discovery of utilitarianism.

That didn't faze my audience at the time because they'd never heard of utilitarianism – the result being that they couldn't make the mistake of believing that it meant resorting to the useful *(utilitaire)*. I explained to them what utilitarianism was in Bentham's work, which is not at all what people think it is. In order to understand it one must read *The Theory of Fictions*.

Utilitarianism means nothing but the following – we must think about the purpose served by the old words, those that already serve us. Nothing more. We must not be surprised by what results when we use them. We know what they are used for – they are used so that there may be the jouissance that should be *(qu'il faut)*. With the caveat that, given the equivocation between *faillir* and *falloir*, the jouissance that should be

---

[19] Eudemonism is the doctrine that the basis of moral obligations is found in the tendency of "right actions" to produce happiness.

must be translated as the jouissance that shouldn't be/never fails *(qu'il ne faut pas)*.[20]

Yes, I am teaching something positive here. Except that it is expressed by a negation. But why shouldn't it be as positive as anything else?

The necessary – what I propose to accentuate for you with this mode – is that which doesn't stop *(ne cesse pas)* what? – being written *(de s'écrire)*.[21] That is a very fine way in which to divide up at least four modal categories. I will explain that to you another time, but I will give you a bit more of a taste this time anyway. "What doesn't stop not being written" is a modal category, and it's not the one you might have expected to be opposed to the necessary, which would have been the contingent. Can you imagine? The necessary is linked *(conjugué)* to the impossible, and this "doesn't stop not being written" is the articulation thereof. What is produced is the jouissance that shouldn't be/could never fail *(qu'il ne faudrait pas)*.[22] That is the correlate of the fact that there's no such thing as a sexual relationship, and it is the substantial aspect *(le substantiel)* of the phallic function.

Let me now return to the textual level. It is the jouissance that shouldn't be/could never fail *(qu'il ne faudrait pas)* – in the conditional tense. That suggests to me that to use it we could employ protasis and apodosis.[23] If it weren't for that, things would go better *(ça irait mieux)* – that's a conditional tense in the second part. That is the material implication, the implication the Stoics realized was perhaps what was most solid in logic.

How are we thus going to express what shouldn't be/could never fail with respect to jouissance, if not by the following? Were there another jouissance than phallic jouissance, it shouldn't be/could never fail to be that one.

56

[20] *Falloir*, used in all the tenses, but only in the third person singular, *il faut, il faudrait*, etc., means "one must," "one should," "one has to," "it is necessary," and so on. *Faillir* means to "fail," "falter," "default," "miss," or "come up short"; in certain contexts, e.g., *j'ai failli faire une gaffe*, "I almost made a blunder," it means to be on the verge of doing something. Both *faillir* and *falloir* are written *faut* in the third person singular, present tense. Hence *la jouissance qu'il ne faut pas* is the jouissance that mustn't be, shouldn't be, but can't fail to be or never fails anyway. (*Faillir* also formerly meant to sin [for a girl], to lapse, or to be remiss in one's commitments.) The phrase *la jouissance qu'il faut* works much better with *falloir* than with *faillir*, because the *il* refers to nothing in particular in the case of the former ("the jouissance that is necessary" or "should be"), whereas it refers to a "he" or an "it" in the case of the latter ("the jouissance that it defaults on" or "the jouissance that he doesn't live up to"). Moreover, for *faillir* to work here grammatically, the phrase would have to be recast: *la jouissance à laquelle il faut.*

[21] *De s'écrire* could also be translated here as "writing itself."

[22] Lacan is playing here on the same equivalence between the verbs *faillir* and *falloir* that he played on two paragraphs back, both verbs being written *faudrait* in the conditional tense, third person singular.

[23] Lacan introduces these terms in his early article, "Logical Time and the Assertion of Anticipated Certainty," where the protasis takes on the meaning of an "if" clause in an if-then type proposition, and the apodosis takes on the meaning of the "then" clause.

That's very nice. One must use things like that, old words, as stupid as anything, but really use them, work them to the bone. That's utilitarianism. And that allowed a giant step to be taken away from the old tales about universals that had preoccupied people since Plato and Aristotle, had dragged along throughout the Middle Ages, and were still suffocating Leibniz, to so great an extent that one wonders how he still managed to be so intelligent.

Were there another one, it shouldn't be/could never fail to be that one.

What does "that one" designate? Does it designate the other in the sentence, or the one on the basis of which we designated that other as other? What I am saying here is sustained at the level of material implication, because the first part designates something false – "Were there another one," but there is no other than phallic jouissance – except the one concerning which woman doesn't breathe a word, perhaps because she doesn't know *(connait)*[24] it, the one that makes her not-whole. It is false that there is another one, but that doesn't stop what follows from being true, namely, that it shouldn't be/could never fail to be that one.

You see that this is entirely correct. When the true is deduced from the false, it is valid. The implication works. The only thing we cannot abide is that from the true should follow the false. Not half bad, this logic stuff! The fact that the Stoics managed to figure that out all by themselves is quite impressive. One mustn't believe that such things bore no relation to jouissance. We have but to rehabilitate the terms to see that.

It is false that there is another. That won't stop me from playing once more on the equivocation based on *faux* (false), by saying that it shouldn't *(faux-drait)* be/could never fail to be/couldn't be false that it is that one.[25] Suppose that there is another – but there isn't. And, simultaneously, it is not because there isn't – and because it is on this that the "it shouldn't be/could never fail" depends – that the cleaver falls any the less on the jouissance with which we began. That one has *(faut)* to be, failing *(faute de)* – you should understand that as guilt – failing the other that is not.[26]

That opens up for us, tangentially, and I am saying this in passing, a little glimpse that has considerable weight in a metaphysics. There may be cases

---

[24] *Connaître* implies something more experiential than *savoir*, and could lead to the following translation here: "she doesn't experience it." Lacan is perhaps also playing on the *con* – the French equivalent for the English slang "cunt" – in *connaître*, and in other verbs as well further on. Cf. his comments in Chapter VI on woman's experience/knowledge of it.

[25] This play on words is untranslatable in English: *faux* ("false" or "wrong") is pronounced in French exactly like the first syllable of *faudrait*.

[26] *Faute de* usually means for lack of or failing that, but here Lacan wants us to also hear the sin or fault in *faute*. Lacan may also want us to hear *faut* at the beginning of the sentence as based on *faillir*: "That one defaults, failing. . . ." The same is perhaps true four paragraphs down.

in which, instead of it being us who go in search of something to reassure ourselves in the manger of metaphysics, we can even give something back to metaphysics. To wit, one must not forget that the fact that nonbeing is not is blamed by speech on being, whose fault it is. It's true that it is its fault, because if being did not exist, we would be far less uneasy with the question of nonbeing, and thus it is deservedly that we reproach being for it, and consider it to be at fault.

That is also why – and this occasionally angers me, it is what I began with, moreover, and I assume you don't remember – when I forget myself *(m'oublie)* to the point of publishing *(p'oublier)*,[27] in other words, of forgetting everything *(tout-blier)* – the whole *(tout)* has something to do with it – I deserve to have to put up with people talking about me and not at all about my book. Which is just like what happened in Milan. Perhaps it wasn't entirely about me that people were speaking when they said that, according to me, ladies don't exist, but it certainly wasn't what I had just said.

In the end, if this jouissance comes to someone *(celui)* who speaks, and not by accident, it is because it is a bit premature. It has something to do with the renowned *(fameux)* sexual relationship, concerning which he will have only too many occasions to realize that it doesn't exist. It is thus second rather than first. There are traces of it in Freud's work. If Freud spoke of *Urverdrängung*, primal repression, it was precisely because the true, good, everyday repression is not first – it is second.

People repress the said jouissance because it is not fitting[28] for it to be spoken, and that is true precisely because the speaking *(dire)* thereof can be no other than the following: qua jouissance, it is inappropriate *(elle ne convient pas)*. I already sustained as much earlier by saying that it is not the one that should be *(faut)*, but the one that shouldn't be/never fails.

Repression is produced only to attest, in all statements *(dires)* and in the slightest statement, to what is implied by the statement that I just enunciated, that jouissance is inappropriate – *non decet*[29] – to the sexual relationship. It is precisely because the said jouissance speaks that the sexual relationship is not.

Which is why that jouissance would do better to hush up, but when it does, that makes the very absence of the sexual relationship a bit harder yet to bear. Which is why, in the final analysis, it doesn't hush up, and why the

[27] *P'oublier* evokes "forgetting" *(oublier)*, "publishing" *(publier)*, and "garbage can" *(poubelle)*.

[28] The French, *il ne convient pas*, can be rendered in a number of ways: it is not "fitting," "suitable," "becoming," "proper," or "appropriate." I translate it in several ways here.

[29] *Non decet* means "not fitting," "not befitting," "not proper," "unbecoming," "unsuitable," etc.

first effect of repression is that it speaks of something else. That is what constitutes the mainspring of metaphor.

There you have it. You see the relationship between all that and utility. It's utilitarian. It makes you capable of serving some purpose, since you don't know (faute de savoir) how to enjoy otherwise than to be enjoyed (être joui) or duped (joué), because it is precisely the jouissance that shouldn't be/could never fail.

4

It's on the basis of this step-by-step approach, which made me "scand"[30] something essential today, that we must consider the light Aristotle and Freud can be seen to shed on each other. We must investigate how what they say (dires) can intersect and cross over into each other's work.

58   In book seven of the Nicomachean Ethics, Aristotle raises the question of pleasure. What seems most certain to him, in referring to jouissance, is no more nor less than the idea that pleasure can but be distinguished from needs, from those needs with which I began in my first sentence, and with which he frames what is at stake in generation. Needs are related to movement. Indeed, Aristotle places at the center of his world – a world that has now definitively disappeared with the tide – the unmoved mover, immediately after which comes the movement it causes, and, a bit further away, what is born and dies, what is engendered and corrupted. That is where needs are situated. Needs are satisfied by movement.

Oddly enough, we find the same thing in Freud's work, but there it concerns the articulation of the pleasure principle. What equivocation makes it such that, according to Freud, the pleasure principle is brought on only by excitation, this excitation provoking movement in order to get away from it? It is strange that that is what Freud enunciates as the pleasure principle, whereas in Aristotle's work, that can only be considered as an attenuation of pain, surely not as a pleasure.

If Aristotle connects the status of pleasure with something, it can only be with what he calls ἐνέργεια, an activity.

Even more oddly, the first example he provides of this, not without coherence, is seeing – it is there that, in his view, resides the supreme pleasure, the one he distinguishes from the level of γένεσις, the generation of some-

---

[30] Scander is the verb form of "scansion," and is usually translated as "to scan" or "scanning" (as in scanning verse). I have opted in all of my translations of Lacan's work to date to introduce a neologism – to scand, scanding – so as to distinguish the far more common contemporary uses of scanning (looking over rapidly, quickly running through a list, taking ultra-thin pictures of the body with a scanner, or "feeding" text and images in digital form into a computer) from Lacan's idea here of cutting, interrupting, punctuating, or highlighting something.

thing, the one that is produced at the heart or center of pure pleasure. No pain has to precede the fact that we see in order for seeing to be a pleasure. It is amusing that having thus posed the question, he has to put forward what? What French cannot translate otherwise, lacking a word that is not equivocal, than by *l'odorer* (smelling). Aristotle here places smell and sight at the same level. As opposed as the second sense seems to be to the first, he tells us that pleasure turns out to be borne thereby. Thirdly, he adds hearing.

It is just about 1:45 p.m. To orient yourselves on the path along which we are proceeding, recall the step we made earlier by formulating that jouissance is centrally related to the one *(celle-là)* that shouldn't be/never fails, that shouldn't be/could never fail in order for there to be a sexual relationship, and remains wholly attached to it. Hence, what emerges with the term by which Aristotle designates it is quite precisely what analytic experience allows us to situate as being the object – from at least one pole of sexual identification, the male pole – the object that puts itself in the place of what cannot be glimpsed of the Other. It is inasmuch as object *a* plays the role somewhere – from a point of departure, a single one, the male one – of that which takes the place of the missing partner, that what we are also used to seeing emerge in the place of the real, namely, fantasy, is constituted.

I almost regret having, in this way, said enough, which always means too much. For one must see the radical difference of what is produced at the other pole, on the basis of woman.

Next time, I will try to enunciate in a way that stands up – and that is complete enough for you to bear the time before we meet again, in other words, half a month – that, for woman – but write woman with the slanted line with which I designate what must be barred – for ~~Woman~~, something other than object *a* is at stake in what comes to make up for *(suppléer)* the sexual relationship that does not exist.

February 13, 1973

VI

God and ~~Woman~~'s jouissance

READING–LOVING, HATING.

MATERIALISTS.

JOUISSANCE OF BEING.

THE MALE, POLYMORPHOUS PERVERT.

MYSTICS.

For a long time I have wanted to speak to you while walking around a bit among you. Thus, I was hoping, I must admit, that the so-called academic vacation would have diminished the number of you attending here.

Since I have been refused this satisfaction, I will return to what I began with the last time – what I called "another satisfaction," the satisfaction of speech.

Another satisfaction is the one that answers to[1] the jouissance that was barely *(juste)* required, just enough *(juste)* for it to happen between what I will abbreviate by calling them man and woman. In other words, the satisfaction that answers to phallic jouissance.

Note here the modification that is introduced by the word "barely" *(juste)*. This "barely" is a "just barely" *(tout juste)*, a "just barely successful" that is the flip-side of failure – it just barely succeeds. This already justifies what Aristotle contributes with the notion of justice as the bare mean *(le juste milieu)*.[2] Perhaps some of you recognized, when I introduced the whole *(tout)* – found in the expression "just barely" *(tout juste)* – that I circumvented the word "prosdiorism,"[3] which designates the whole that is not lacking in any language. Well, the fact that it is the prosdiorism, the whole, that allows us on this occasion to slide from Aristotle's justice to the just barely *(justesse)*, to the just barely successful *(réussite de justesse)*, is what

[1] The French here, *répond à*, can mean a number of different things: "responds to," "corresponds to," "answers to," "talks back to," and so on. It is found again in the next sentence.

[2] Aristotle defines justice as the intermediate point or mean between two extremes in *Nicomachean Ethics*, Book V, Chapters 3–5. I have changed the more standard translations – "golden mean" or "happy medium" – to convey Lacan's sense here of what "just barely" achieves the middle position.

[3] Lacan uses this term repeatedly in Seminar XIX (December 8, 1971, January 12 and 19, 1972, etc.) in reference to what have come to be known as the existential and universal quantifiers. They appear in Aristotle's work as "one," "some," "all," and the negations of these terms.

legitimates my having brought in Aristotle's work here. Indeed – right? – it cannot be understood immediately like that.

If Aristotle cannot be understood so easily, due to the distance that separates us from him, that is what, in my view, justifies my saying to you that reading in no way obliges you to understand. You have to read first.

1   62

That is why today, in a way that may seem paradoxical to certain of you, I will advise you to read a book regarding which the least one can say is that it concerns me. The book is entitled *Le titre de la lettre*,[4] and was published by the Galilée publishing company, in the collection *A la lettre*. I won't tell you who the authors are – they seem to me to be no more than pawns in this case.

That is not to diminish their work, for I will say that, personally, I read it with the greatest satisfaction. I would like you to put yourselves to the test of this book, written with the worst of intentions, as you will easily see in the last thirty pages. I cannot encourage its circulation strongly enough.

I can say in a certain way that, if it is a question of reading, I have never been so well read – with so much love. Of course, as is attested to by the end of the book, it is a love about which the least one can say is that its usual underside *(doublure)* in analytic theory need not be ruled out here.

But that goes too far. To even talk about subjects in this case, in any way whatsoever, may be going too far. To even mention their feelings is perhaps to recognize them too much as subjects.

Let us simply say that it is a model of good reading, such good reading that I can safely say that I regret never having obtained anything like it from my closest associates. The authors felt that they had to limit themselves – and, well, why not compliment them for it, since the condition of a reading is obviously that it impose limits on itself – to an article included in my *Écrits* that is entitled "The Instance of the Letter."

Beginning with what distinguishes me from Saussure, and what made me, as they say, distort him, we proceed, little by little, to the impasse I designate concerning analytic discourse's approach to truth and its paradoxes. That is, no doubt, something that ultimately escapes – I needn't probe any further – those who set themselves this extraordinary task. It is as if it were precisely upon reaching the impasse to which my discourse is designed to lead them that they considered their work done, declaring themselves – or rather declaring me, which amounts to the same thing given

---

[4] In English, see Jean-Luc Nancy and Philippe Lacoue-Labarthe, *The Title of the Letter,* translated by David Pettigrew and François Raffoul (Albany: SUNY Press, 1992).

their conclusions – confounded. It would be altogether appropriate for you yourselves to examine their conclusions, which, you will see, can be qualified as inconsiderate. Up until these conclusions, the work proceeds in a way that I can only characterize as strikingly illuminating *(éclaircissement)*. If it could, by any chance, lighten your attendance here *(éclaircir)*,[5] I would regard that as merely an added perk for me, but, after all, I'm not sure – why not have faith in you *(vous faire confiance)*, since there are always just as many of you here? – whether anything could put you off.[6]

Thus, apart from the last twenty or thirty pages – to tell you the truth, those are the only ones I skimmed through – the others will be a comfort to you that, overall, I can but wish you.

2

On that note, I will continue with what I have to say to you today, namely, to further articulate the consequence of the fact that no relationship gets constituted between the sexes in the case of speaking beings, for it is on that basis alone that what makes up for that relationship can be enunciated.

For a long time I have scanded what constitutes the first step in this undertaking with a certain "There's such a thing as One" *(Y a d' l'Un)*. This "There's such a thing as One" is not simple – that's the word for it. In psychoanalysis, or more precisely in Freud's discourse, it is announced by the fact that Eros is defined as the fusion that makes one from two, as what is supposed to gradually tend in the direction of making but one from an immense multitude. But, since it is clear that even all of you – as numerous as you are here, assuredly forming a multitude – not only do not make one, but have no chance of pulling that off – which is only too amply demonstrated every day, if only by communing in my speech – Freud obviously has to bring in another factor that poses an obstacle to this universal Eros in the guise of Thanatos, the reduction to dust.

That is obviously a metaphor that Freud is able to use thanks to the fortunate discovery of the two units of the germ *(germen)*, the ovum and the spermatozoon, about which one could roughly say that it is on the basis of their fusion that is engendered what? A new being. Except that that doesn't happen without meiosis, a thoroughly obvious subtraction, at least for one of the two, just before the very moment at which the conjunction occurs, a subtraction of certain elements that are not superfluous in the final operation.

[5] Lacan is playing here on the double meaning of *éclaircir*, which he used in the first sentence of this class in the sense of "diminishing" (the number of those attending his lecture); it also means to "enlighten."
[6] The French here, *je ne suis pas sûr . . . que rien enfin ne vous rebute*, could perhaps also mean "I'm not sure . . . whether there is nothing that could put you off."

But biological metaphors clearly cannot reassure us here – they reassure us here still less than elsewhere. If the unconscious is truly what I say it is, being structured like a language, it is at the level of language *(langue)* that we must investigate this One. The course of the centuries has provided this One with an infinite resonance. Need I mention here the Neo-Platonists? Perhaps I will have occasion to mention their adventure very quickly later, since what I need to do today is very precisely designate from whence the thing not only may but must be taken up on the basis of our discourse and of the revamping our experience brings about in the realm of Eros.

We must begin with the fact that this "There's such a thing as One" is to be understood in the sense that there's One all alone *(il y a de l'Un tout seul)*. We can grasp, thereby, the crux *(nerf)* of what we must clearly call by the name by which the thing resounds throughout the centuries, namely, love.

In analysis, we deal with nothing but that, and analysis doesn't operate by any other pathway. It is a singular pathway in that it alone allowed us to isolate what I, I who am talking to you, felt I needed to base transference on, insofar as it is not distinguished from love, that is, on the formulation "the subject supposed to know."

I cannot but mention the new resonance this term "knowledge" can take on for you. I love the person I assume to have knowledge. Earlier you saw me stall, back off, and hesitate to come down on one side or the other, on the side of love or on the side of what we call hatred, when I insistently invited you to read a book whose climax is expressly designed to discredit me *(déconsidérer)* – which is certainly not something that can be backed away from by someone who speaks, ultimately, but on the basis of "desideration"[7] and aims at nothing else. The fact is that this climax appears sustainable to the authors precisely where there is a "desupposition" of my knowledge. If I said that they hate me it is because they "desuppose" that I have knowledge.

And why not? Why not, if it turns out that that must be the condition for what I call reading? After all, what can I presume Aristotle knew? Perhaps the less I assume he has knowledge, the better I read him. That is the condition of a strict putting to the test of reading, a condition I don't weasel out of.

What is offered to us to be read by that aspect of language that exists, namely, what is woven as an effect of its erosion[8] – that is how I define what is written thereof – cannot be ignored. Thus, it would be disdainful not

[7] "Sideration" is a medical term for the sudden annihilation of the vital functions due to an intense emotional shock. In French, it is related to *sidérer*, "to stun," "stagger," or "shock." *Dé-sidération* is close in spelling to *déconsidérer*, used earlier in the sentence.
[8] The French here, *ce qui vient à se tramer d'effet de son ravinement,* is rather ambiguous.

to at least recall to mind what has been said about love throughout the ages by a thought that has called itself – improperly, I must say – philosophical.

I am not going to provide a general review of the question here. It seems to me that, given the type of faces I see all around the room, you must have heard that, in philosophy, the love of God *(l'amour de Dieu)*[9] has occupied a certain place. We have here a sweeping fact that analytic discourse cannot but take into account, if only tangentially.

I will recall to mind here something that was said after I was, as the authors express themselves in this booklet, "excluded" from Sainte-Anne [Hospital]. In fact, I was not excluded; I withdrew. That's a horse of a different color, especially given the importance of the term "excluded" in my topology – but it's of no import, since that's not what we're here to talk about. Well-intentioned people – who are far worse than ill-intentioned ones – were surprised when they heard that I situated a certain Other between man and woman that certainly seemed like the good old God of time immemorial. It was only an echo, but they made themselves the unpaid conduits thereof. They were, by God, it must be admitted, from the pure philosophical tradition, and among those who claim to be materialists – that is why I say "pure," for there is nothing more philosophical than materialism. Materialism believes that it is obliged, God only knows why – a serendipitous expression here – to be on its guard against this God who, as I said, dominated the whole debate regarding love in philosophy. Those people, to whose warm reception I owed a renewed audience, thus manifested a certain uneasiness.

It seems clear to me that the Other – put forward at the time of "The Instance of the Letter" as the locus of speech – was a way, I can't say of laicizing, but of exorcising the good old God. After all, there are even people[10] who complimented me for having been able to posit in one of my last seminars that God doesn't exist. Obviously, they hear *(entendent)*[11] – they hear, but alas, they understand, and what they understand is a bit precipitate.

So today, I am instead going to show you in what sense the good old God exists. The way in which he exists will not necessarily please everyone, especially not the theologians, who are, as I have been saying for a long time, far more capable than I am of doing without his existence. I, unfortunately, am not entirely in the same position, because I deal with the Other.

---

[9] The French here could also mean "God's love."

[10] The French here, *il y a bien des gens,* could also be translated as "there are plenty of people."

[11] *Entendre* means both "to hear" and "to understand"; here, however, it is being juxtaposed with *comprendre,* which I have translated as "to understand" in the latter part of this sentence.

This Other – assuming there is but one all alone – must have some relationship with what appears of the other sex.

On that score, I didn't stop myself, the year I mentioned last time, that of *The Ethics of Psychoanalysis,* from referring to courtly love. What is courtly love?

It is a highly refined way of making up for *(suppléer à)* the absence of the sexual relationship, by feigning that we are the ones who erect an obstacle thereto. It is truly the most amazing thing that has even been attempted. But how can one denounce the fake?

Rather than dwelling on the paradox of why courtly love appeared during the feudal era, materialists should see therein a magnificent occasion to show, on the contrary, how it is rooted in the discourse of loyalty *(féalité),* of fidelity to the person. In the final analysis, the "person" always has to do with the master's discourse. Courtly love is, for man – in relation to whom the lady is entirely, and in the most servile sense of the word, a subject – the only way to elegantly pull off the absence of the sexual relationship.

It is along this pathway that I shall deal – later though, for today I must break new ground – with the notion of the obstacle, with what in Aristotle's work – whatever else may be said, I prefer Aristotle to Jaufré Rudel[12] – is precisely called the obstacle, ἔνστασις.[13]

My readers – whose book you must, I repeat, all go out and buy later – even found that. They investigate the instance so thoroughly, so carefully – as I said, I have never seen a single one of my students do such work, alas, no one will ever take seriously what I write, except of course those about whom I said earlier that they hate me in the guise of desupposing my knowledge – that they even discover the ἔνστασις, the Aristotelian logical obstacle that I had reserved for the end. It is true that they do not see where it fits in. But they are so used to working, especially when something motivates them – the desire, for example, to obtain their Master's,[14] a truly serendipitous term here – that they even mention that in the footnote on pages 28 and 29.[15]

Consult Aristotle and you will know everything when I at last come to

66

---

[12] A reference to the courtly love poet, Jaufré Rudel de Blaye. See *Les chansons de Jaufré Rudel,* edited by Alfred Jeanroy (Paris: Librairie Ancienne Honoré Champion, 1924). In English, see, for example, *Trobador Poets,* translated by Barbara Smythe (New York: Cooper Square Publishers, 1966), and *Songs of the Troubadours,* translated by Anthony Bonner (New York: Schocken Books, 1972).
[13] ἔνστασις is the obstacle one raises to an adversary's argument; it is also the exception to a universal predicate, hence an instance or counterinstance that refutes a general claim. This is but one example of the inappropriateness of translating Lacan's *"Instance de la lettre"* as "Agency of the Letter."
[14] The French term, *maîtrise,* means both "Master's degree" (in arts or sciences) and "mastery."
[15] This corresponds to footnote 4 on page 24 of the English edition.

this business of the ἔνστασις. You can read, one after the other, the passage in the *Rhetoric* and the two sections of the *Topics*[16] that will allow you to truly know what I mean when I try to integrate my four formulas, $\exists x\overline{\Phi x}$ and the rest, into Aristotle's work.

Lastly, to finish up on this point, why should materialists, as they are called, be indignant about the fact that I situate – and why shouldn't I – God as the third party in this business of human love? Even materialists sometimes know a bit about the *ménage à trois*, don't they?

So let us try to push ahead. Let us try to push ahead regarding what results from the following, that nothing indicates that I don't know what I'm saying when I speak to you. What creates a problem right from the beginning of this book, which continues right up until the end, is that it assumes – and with that one can do anything – that I have an ontology, or, what amounts to the same thing, a system.

In the circular diagram[17] in which is supposedly laid out what I put forward regarding the instance of the letter, the authors are at least honest enough to use dotted lines – for good reason, since they hardly weigh anything – to situate all of my statements enveloping the names of the principal philosophers into whose general ontology I am claimed to insert my supposed system. But it cannot be ambiguous that I oppose to the concept of being – as it is sustained in the philosophical tradition, that is, as rooted in the very thinking that is supposed to be its correlate – the notion that we are duped (*joués*)[18] by jouissance.

Thought is jouissance. What analytic discourse contributes is the following, and it is already hinted at in the philosophy of being: there is jouissance of being.

I spoke to you of the *Nicomachean Ethics* because the trace is there. What Aristotle wanted to know, and that paved the way for everything that followed in his wake, is what the jouissance of being is. Saint Thomas had no problem after that coming up with the physical theory of love – as it was called by the abbot Rousselot, whom I mentioned last time[19] – namely, that the first being we have a sense of is clearly our being, and everything that is for the good of our being must, by dint of this very fact, be the Supreme Being's jouissance, that is, God's. To put it plainly, by loving God, we love

---

[16] Lacan is referring here to the passages in Aristotle's work mentioned in the footnote of *The Title of the Letter: Rhetoric* II, 25, 1402a, *Topics* VIII, 2, 157ab, and II, 11, 115b. The authors also mention *Prior Analytics* II, 26.

[17] Found on page 112 (page 110 of the English edition), and entitled " 'System' of 'The Instance of the Letter,' or *De revolutionibus orbium litteralium*."

[18] The French here literally means "played"; figuratively it means "deceived," "had," "toyed with," "outsmarted," and so on.

[19] See Pierre Rousselot, *Pour l'histoire du problème de l'amour au moyen âge* (Münster: Aschendorffsche Buchhandlung, 1907). Lacan did not mention Rousselot in the last class as published in this Seminar.

ourselves, and by first loving ourselves – "well-ordered charity," as it is put[20] – we pay the appropriate homage to God.

Being – if people want me to use this term at all costs – the being that I oppose to that – and to which this little volume is forced to attest right from the very first pages of its reading, which simply involve reading – is the being of signifierness. And I fail to see in what sense I am stooping to the ideals of materialism – I say "to the ideals" because they're beyond its scope – when I identify the reason for the being of signifierness in jouissance, jouissance of the body.

But, you see, a body hasn't seemed materialistic enough since Democritus. One has to find atoms and the whole nine yards, not to mention sight, smell, and everything that follows therefrom. All that goes together.

It's no accident that Aristotle occasionally quotes Democritus, even if he feigns disgust when he does so, for he relies on the latter's work. In fact, the atom is simply an element of flying signifierness, quite simply a $\sigma\tau o\iota\chi\hat{\epsilon}\iota o\nu$.[21] Except that it is extremely difficult to make it work out right when one retains only what makes the element an element, namely, the fact that it is unique, whereas one should introduce the other a little bit, namely, difference.

Now, if there's no such thing as a sexual relationship, we must see in what respect the jouissance of the body can serve a purpose here.

3

Let us approach things first from the pole at which every x is a function of Φx, that is, from the pole where man is situated.

One ultimately situates oneself there by choice – women are free to situate themselves there if it gives them pleasure to do so. Everyone knows there are phallic women, and that the phallic function doesn't stop men from being homosexuals. It is, nevertheless, the phallic function that helps them situate themselves as men and approach woman. I shall discuss man quickly, because what I have to talk about today is woman and because I assume that I have already sufficiently hammered it home to you[22] that you still recall the following – there is no chance for a man to have jouissance of

20 "*Charité bien ordonnée commence par soi-même*" is a well-known French proverb. In English, it literally means "Well-ordered charity begins with oneself," but the most closely related proverb in English is "Charity begins at home."

21 $\sigma\tau o\iota\chi\hat{\epsilon}\iota o\nu$ means "element," "principal constituent," "letter," or "part of speech."

22 Lacan had already devoted a great deal of attention in Seminars XVIII and XIX to the phallic function and the four logical formulas he quickly glosses below; that is what allows him to assume that his audience still recalls what he has already stated about man.

a woman's body, otherwise stated, for him to make love, without castration (*à moins de castration*),[23] in other words, without something that says no to the phallic function.

That is the result of analytic experience. That doesn't stop him from desiring woman in every way, even when that condition does not obtain. He not only desires her, but does all kinds of things to her that bear an astonishing resemblance to love.

As opposed to what Freud maintains, it is man – I mean he who happens to be male without knowing what to do with it, all the while being a speaking being – who approaches woman, or who can believe that he approaches her, because on that score there is no dearth of convictions, the *con-victions* I spoke about last time.[24] But what he approaches is the cause of his desire that I have designated as object *a*. That is the act of love.[25] To make love (*faire l'amour*), as the very expression indicates, is poetry.[26] But there is a world between poetry and the act. The act of love is the male's polymorphous perversion, in the case of speaking beings. There is nothing more certain, coherent, and rigorous as far as Freudian discourse is concerned.

I still have a half hour to try to thrust you, if I dare express myself thus,[27] into how things stand at woman's pole. One of the following two things is true: either what I write has no meaning at all – which is, by the way, the conclusion of the short book [discussed earlier], and that is why I beg you to have a look at it – or when I write $\overline{\forall}x\Phi x$, a never-before-seen function in which the negation is placed on the quantifier, which should be read "not-whole," it means that when any speaking being whatsoever situates itself under the banner "women," it is on the basis of the following – that it grounds itself as being not-whole in situating itself in the phallic function.[28] That is what defines what? Woman precisely, except that Woman can only be written with a bar through it.[29] There's no such thing as Woman, Woman with a capital *W* indicating the universal. There's no such thing as

68

---

[23] The French here might also be translated as "anything less than (or short of) castration" or as "with something less than (or in the case of something less than) castration." See the last paragraph of this chapter.
[24] Lacan is referring back to the *con-vaincu* he mentioned in the last lecture, the vanquished (or convinced) asshole or idiot. In the play on words, *con* as "cunt" may also be intended.
[25] The French here, *l'acte d'amour,* seems to imply "the act of love-making," more than a "loving act." Hence it strikes me as more or less equivalent here to *l'acte sexuel,* i.e., intercourse.
[26] *Faire,* in French, often suggests something more make-believe than "make" in English. The hysteric who *fait l'homme* plays the part or role of man, perhaps like an actor. *Faire l'amour* can thus suggest something like "playing at love" or "creating love."
[27] *Introduire,* which I have translated here as "thrust," can take on the meaning of penetration in certain contexts.
[28] Or "it grounds itself as not-wholly situating itself in the phallic function."
[29] In the French, Lacan says that we must bar the article *"La"* in *"La femme,"* which, as he tells us in the next sentence, is the definite article that designates the

Woman because, in her essence – I've already risked using that term, so why should I think twice about using it again? – she is not-whole.

I see my students far less attached to reading my work than the slightest underling when he is motivated by the desire to obtain a Master's; not one of them has avoided producing an utter and complete muddle regarding the lack of a signifier, the signifier of the lack of a signifier, and other gibberish regarding the phallus, whereas with "woman" (la) I am designating for you the signifier that is, nevertheless, common and even indispensable. The proof is that, earlier, I already spoke of man and "woman" (la femme). That "woman" (la) is a signifier. With it I symbolize the signifier whose place it is indispensable to mark – that place cannot be left empty. "Woman" (la) is a signifier, the crucial property (propre) of which is that it is the only one that cannot signify anything, and this is simply because it grounds woman's status in the fact that she is not-whole. That means we can't talk about Woman (La femme).

A woman can but be excluded[30] by the nature of things, which is the nature of words, and it must be said that if there is something that women themselves complain about enough for the time being, that's it. It's just that they don't know what they're saying – that's the whole difference between them and me.

The fact remains that if she is excluded by the nature of things, it is precisely in the following respect: being not-whole, she has a supplementary jouissance compared to what the phallic function designates by way of jouissance.

You will notice that I said "supplementary." If I had said "complementary" what a mess we'd be in! We would fall back into the whole.

Women content themselves (s'en tiennent),[31] any woman contents herself (aucune s'en tient), being not-whole, with the jouissance in question and, well, generally speaking, we would be wrong not to see that, contrary to what people say, it is nevertheless they who possess men.

Commoners – I know some of them, they're not necessarily here, but I know quite a few – commoners call their wife "la bourgeoise." That's what that means. He is the one who obeys orders (à la botte), not her. Since Rabelais, we have known that the phallus, her man, as she says, is not indif-

69

---

universal. In English, the definite article "the" sometimes functions in that way, as in "the Good," "the Just," and so on. In the case of woman, however, "the woman" seems to imply a specific woman ("the woman of one's dreams," "the woman downstairs"), whereas Lacan is aiming here instead at a universal like womanliness or the essence of woman. See, on this point, Chapter I, footnote 28.

[30] Il n'y a de femme qu'exclue could also be rendered as "There is no woman except excluded."

[31] This could be translated in many ways: "Women confine themselves . . . to the jouissance in question," "Women stick . . . to . . . ," "Women go . . . with . . . ," etc.

ferent to her. But, and this is the whole point, she has different ways of approaching that phallus and of keeping it for herself. It's not because she is not-wholly in the phallic function that she is not there at all. She is *not* not at all there.[32] She is there in full (*à plein*). But there is something more (*en plus*).

Be careful with this "more" – beware of taking it too far too quickly. I cannot designate it any better or otherwise because I have to rough it out (*trancher*),[33] and I have to go quickly.

There is a jouissance, since I am confining myself here to jouissance,[34] a jouissance of the body that is, if I may express myself thus – why not make a book title out of it? it'll be the next book in the Galilée collection – "beyond the phallus." That would be cute, huh? And it would give another consistency to the women's liberation movement. A jouissance beyond the phallus. . . .

You may have noticed – I am naturally speaking here to the few semblances of men I see here and there, fortunately I don't know them for the most part, and that way I don't presume anything about the others – that now and then, there is something that, for a brief moment, shakes (*secoue*) women up or rescues them (*secourt*). When you look up the etymology of those two words in the Bloch et Von Wartburg that is so delectable to me, and that I am sure you don't even all have on your bookshelves, you'll see the relationship between them.[35] Such things don't happen by chance, all the same.

There is a jouissance that is hers (*à elle*), that belongs to that "she" (*elle*) that doesn't exist and doesn't signify anything.[36] There is a jouissance that is hers about which she herself perhaps knows nothing if not that she experiences it – that much she knows. She knows it, of course, when it comes (*arrive*). It doesn't happen (*arrive*) to all of them.

I don't want to end up talking about putative frigidity, but one must isolate that aspect of relationships between men and women that is related to current trends (*la mode*). It's very important. Of course in Freud's discourse, alas, as in courtly love, all of that is covered over by minute consid-

_____ [32] This is an obvious commentary on Lacan's second matheme for women: $\exists x \Phi x$.

[33] *Trancher* literally means to "cut or slice"; figuratively it means "to decide, determine, or settle (a debate or question)." Lacan's concern here seems to be to simply lay down a few guideposts at the outset.

[34] Lacan uses the same expression here, *s'en tenir à la jouissance*, as he did at the beginning of the third paragraph back.

[35] The two verbs, *secouer* and *secourir*, are discussed on page 581 of the *Dictionnaire étymologique de la langue française*, by Oscar Bloch and Walther von Wartburg (Paris: Presses Universitaires de France, 1932).

[36] This is, perhaps, a reference to what Lacan says elsewhere: "The so-called third person [he, she, or it] doesn't exist" (Seminar III, *The Psychoses*, translated by Russell Grigg [New York: Norton, 1993], p. 314).

erations that have led to all kinds of problems (*ravages*). Minute
considerations concerning clitoral jouissance and the jouissance that people
call by whatever name they can find, the other one, precisely, the one that
I am trying to get you to approach by a logical pathway, because, as things
currently stand, there is no other.

The plausibility of what I am claiming here – namely, that woman knows
nothing of this jouissance – is underscored by the fact that in all the time
people have been begging them, begging them on their hands and knees –
I spoke last time of women psychoanalysts – to try to tell us, not a word!
We've never been able to get anything out of them. So we call this jouissance
by whatever name we can come up with, "vaginal," and speak of the poste-
rior pole of the uterine orifice and other such "cunt-torsions" (*conneries*) –   70
that's the word for it! If she simply experienced it and knew nothing about
it, that would allow us to cast myriad doubts on this notorious (*fameuse*)
frigidity.

That too is a theme, a literary theme. And it's worth dwelling on for a
moment. I've been doing nothing but that since I was twenty, exploring the
philosophers on the subject of love. Naturally, I didn't immediately focus
on the question of love, but that did dawn on me at one point, with the
abbot Rousselot, actually, whom I mentioned earlier, and the whole quarrel
about physical love and ecstatic love, as they are called.[37] I understand why
Gilson didn't find that opposition to be a very good one.[38] He thought
that Rousselot had made a discovery that wasn't really one, because that
opposition was part of the problem, and love is just as ecstatic in Aristotle's
work as in Saint Bernard's,[39] assuming one knows how to read the chapters
regarding φιλία, friendship. Some of you must surely know what literary
debauchery occurred around that: Denis de Rougemont – have a look at
Love in the Western World,[40] it gets red hot! – and then another no stupider
than anyone else, named Nygren, a Protestant, [the author of] *Agape and*

[37] See *Écrits*, 119, and Seminar III, 287. Rousselot explains that "physical
love" was not understood in the Middle Ages as corporal or bodily, but rather as
natural love – the kind of love one finds in nature between mother bear and cub, for
example (*Pour l'histoire du problème d'amour au moyen âge*, p. 3). In the translation of
Saint Thomas Acquinas' *Summa Theologica* prepared by the Fathers of the English
Dominican Province, it is rendered as "natural love" (Chicago: Encyclopedia Bri-
tannica, 1952) (Question 60).
[38] See Étienne-Henri Gilson, *The Choir of Muses* (*L'École des muses*), 1951.
[39] Lacan is, no doubt, referring here to Bernard of Clairvaux, a Cistercian;
see *Bernard of Clairvaux: Selected Works*, translated by G.R. Evans (New York: Paulist Press, 1987).
[40] This book was published in French in 1939 as *L'Amour et l'Occident*. It was
translated into English by Montgomery Belgion and published simultaneously in
the U.S. and England under different titles: *Love in the Western World* (New York:
Pantheon, 1940 and 1956) and *Passion and Society* (London: Faber and Faber Ltd.,
1940 and 1956).

Eros.[41] Christianity naturally ended up inventing a God such that he is the one who gets off (*jouit*)!

There is, nevertheless, a little connection when you read certain serious authors, like women, as if by chance. I will give you a reference here to an author, a reference I owe to a very nice person who had read the author's work and brought it to me. I read it immediately. I'd better write her name on the board, otherwise you won't buy it. It is Hadewijch d'Anvers, a Beguine – she is what we so quaintly refer to as a mystic.[42]

I don't use the word "mystic" as Péguy did.[43] Mysticism isn't everything that isn't politics. It is something serious, about which several people inform us – most often women, or bright people like Saint John of the Cross, because one is not obliged, when one is male, to situate oneself on the side of ∀xΦx. One can also situate oneself on the side of the not-whole. There are men who are just as good as women. It happens. And who also feel just fine about it. Despite – I won't say their phallus – despite what encumbers them that goes by that name, they get the idea or sense that there must be a jouissance that is beyond. Those are the ones we call mystics.

I have already spoken about other people who were not too bad in terms of mysticism, but who were situated instead on the side of the phallic function, Angelus Silesius, for example.[44] Confusing his contemplative eye with the eye with which God looks at him, must, if kept up, partake of perverse jouissance. For the Hadewijch in question, it's like for Saint Teresa – you need but go to Rome and see the statue by Bernini[45] to immediately understand that she's coming. There's no doubt about it. What is she getting off on? It is clear that the essential testimony of the mystics consists in saying that they experience it, but know nothing about it.

These mystical jaculations are neither idle chatter nor empty verbiage; they provide, all in all, some of the best reading one can find – at the bottom of the page, drop a footnote, "Add to that list Jacques Lacan's *Écrits*," because it's of the same order. Thanks to which, naturally, you are all going

71

---

[41] Anders Nygren's *Agape and Eros,* translated by Philip S. Watson (Philadelphia: Westminster Press, 1953); partial translations were published in England between 1932 and 1939 by the S.P.C.K. House. Originally published in Swedish as *Den Kristna Kärlekstanken genom tiderna. Eros och Agape* (Stockholm: Svenska Kyrkans Diakonistyrelses Bokförlag, 1930 and 1936).

[42] See, in particular, *Hadewijch: The Complete Works,* translated by Mother Columba Hart (New York: Paulist Press, 1980).

[43] See Charles Péguy, *Notre Patrie* (1905), *Notre Jeunesse* (1910), and *Mystère de la charité de Jeanne d'Arc* (1910).

[44] See, in particular, *Angelus Silesius: The Cherubinic Wanderer,* translated by Maria Shrady (New York: Paulist Press, 1986).

[45] "The Ecstasy of St. Teresa" is a marble and gilded bronze niche sculpture by Gian Lorenzo Bernini (1645–52) located in the Coronaro Chapel in Santa Maria della Vittoria in Rome. See the cover photo of the French edition of this Seminar.

to be convinced that I believe in God. I believe in the jouissance of woman insofar as it is extra (*en plus*), as long as you put a screen in front of this "extra" until I have been able to properly explain it.

What was attempted at the end of the last century, in Freud's time, what all sorts of decent souls around Charcot and others were trying to do, was to reduce mysticism to questions of cum (*affaires de foutre*). If you look closely, that's not it at all. Doesn't this jouissance one experiences and yet knows nothing about put us on the path of ex-sistence? And why not interpret one face of the Other, the God face, as based on feminine jouissance?

As all of that is produced thanks to the being of signifierness, and as that being has no other locus than the locus of the Other (*Autre*) that I designate with capital *A*, one sees the "cross-sightedness"[46] that results. And as that is also where the father function is inscribed, insofar as castration is related to the father function, we see that that doesn't make two Gods (*deux Dieu*), but that it doesn't make just one either.

In other words, it's no accident that Kierkegaard discovered existence in a seducer's little love affair. It's by castrating himself, by giving up love, that he thinks he will accede to it.[47] But perhaps, after all – why not? – Regine too existed. This desire for a good at one remove (*au second degré*), a good that is not caused by a little *a* – perhaps it was through Regine that he attained that dimension.

February 20, 1973

[46] *Biglerie* literally means cross-eyedness, and seems to connote a sort of hoodwinking based on double-vision.

[47] "It" here seems to refer to "existence." See, in particular, Soren Kierkegaard, *The Diary of a Seducer* (New York: Frederick Ungar, 1966).

VII

A love letter *(une lettre d'âmour)*

COALESCENCE AND SCISSION OF *a* AND S(Ⱥ).

THE BEYONDSEX.

SPEAKING TO NO AVAIL.

PSYCHOANALYSIS IS NOT A COSMOLOGY.

KNOWLEDGE OF JOUISSANCE.

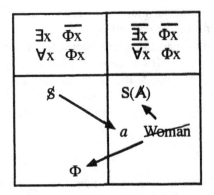

After what I just put on the board, you may think you know everything. Don't.

Today I am going to try to speak about knowledge, about that knowledge which, in the inscription of the four discourses – on which the social link is based, as I thought I could show you – I symbolized by writing S_2. Perhaps I will manage today to make you sense why this 2 goes further than a secondariness in relation to the pure signifier that is written S_1.

1

Since I decided to give you this inscription as a prop on the blackboard, I am going to comment on it, briefly I hope. I did not, I must admit, write it down or prepare it anywhere.[1] It doesn't strike me as exemplary, if not, as usual, in producing misunderstandings.

74   In effect, a discourse like analytic discourse aims at meaning. By way of

---

[1] It should be noted that the top four formulas in the table had already been presented by Lacan in Seminars XVIII and XIX.

meaning, it is clear that I can only deliver to you, to each of you, what you are already on the verge of absorbing. That has a limit, a limit provided by the meaning in which you live. I wouldn't be exaggerating if I said that that doesn't go very far. What analytic discourse brings out is precisely the idea that that meaning is based on semblance *(ce sens est du semblant).*[2]

If analytic discourse indicates that that meaning is sexual, that can only be by explaining its limit. There is nowhere any kind of a last word if not in the sense in which "word" is "not a word" *(mot, c'est motus)*[3] – I have already stressed that. "No answer, not a word" *(Pas de réponse, mot)*, La Fontaine says somewhere. Meaning *(sens)* indicates the direction toward which it fails *(échoue).*[4]

Having posited that, which should make you beware understanding too quickly, having taken all these precautions dictated by mere prudence – φρόνησις, as it is expressed in Greek in which so many things were said, but which remained far from what analytic discourse allows us to articulate – here is more or less what is inscribed on the blackboard.

We'll start with the four propositional formulas at the top of the table, two of which lie to the left, the other two to the right. Every speaking being situates itself on one side or the other. On the left, the lower line – $\forall x \Phi x$ – indicates that it is through the phallic function that man as whole acquires his inscription *(prend son inscription)*,[5] with the proviso that this function is limited due to the existence of an x by which the function Φx is negated *(niée)*: $\exists x \overline{\Phi x}$. That is what is known as the father function[6] – whereby we find, via negation, the proposition $\overline{\Phi x}$, which grounds the operativity *(exercice)* of what makes up for the sexual relationship with castration, insofar as that relationship is in no way inscribable. The whole here is thus based on

---

[2] The French, *semblant,* was still in currency in English in Carlyle's time; see his *Heroes* (1841), verse 284: "Thou art not *true;* thou art not extant, only semblant." It took on the meanings of seeming, apparent, and counterfeit, meanings still associated with the contemporary English "semblance." Jacques-Alain Miller proposes the term "make-believe" to render it in "Microscopia: An Introduction to the Reading of *Television*" (translated by Bruce Fink) in Jacques Lacan, *Television: A Challenge to the Psychoanalytic Establishment,* edited by Joan Copjec (New York: Norton, 1990). Here I have generally preferred "semblance"; in the instance at hand, Lacan says *du semblant,* implying either "some semblance" (like some water) or "based on semblance." On semblance see, above all, Lacan's Seminar XVIII, *D'un discours qui ne serait pas du semblant* ("On a Discourse That Would Not Be Based on Semblance").

[3] *Motus* might also be translated as "don't breathe a word of it" or "mum's the word."

[4] *Sens* in French also means "direction."

[5] The French here could perhaps also be rendered as "can be written." *Inscription* in French also means "enrollment," "registration," and "matriculation."

[6] The French here, *la fonction du père,* could also be translated as "the father's function" or "the function of the father."

the exception posited as the end-point *(terme)*, that is, on that which alto-gether negates Φx.

On the other side, you have the inscription of the woman portion of speaking beings. Any speaking being whatsoever, as is expressly formulated in Freudian theory, whether provided with the attributes of masculinity – attributes that remain to be determined – or not, is allowed to inscribe itself in this part. If it inscribes itself there, it will not allow for any universality – it will be a not-whole, insofar as it has the choice of positing itself in Φx or of not being there *(de n'en pas être)*.[7]

Those are the only possible definitions of the so-called man or woman portion for that which finds itself in the position of inhabiting language.

Underneath – that is, below the horizontal bar where the vertical bar *(division)* is crossed over, that division of what is improperly called human-ity insofar as humanity is divided up into sexual identifications – you have a scanded indication of what is in question. On the side of man, I have inscribed $, certainly not to privilege him in any way, and the Φ that props him[8] up as signifier and is also incarnated in S_1, which, of all the signifiers, is the signifier for which there is no signified, and which, with respect to meaning *(sens)*, symbolizes the failure thereof. It is "half-sense," "inde-sense" *par excellence*, or if you will allow me again, "reti-sense." This $, thus doubled by that signifier on which, in the end, it does not even depend, this $ never deals with anything by way of a partner but object *a* inscribed on the other side of the bar. He is unable to attain his sexual partner, who is the Other, except inasmuch as his partner is the cause of his desire. In this respect, as is indicated elsewhere in my graphs by the oriented conjunc-tion of $ and *a*, this is nothing other than fantasy. This fantasy, in which the subject is caught up *(pris)*, is as such the basis of what is expressly called the "reality principle" in Freudian theory.

Now for the other side. What I am working on this year is what Freud expressly left aside: *Was will das Weib?* "What does woman want?" Freud claims that there is only masculine libido.[9] What does that mean if not that a field that certainly is not negligible is thus ignored. That field is the one of all beings that take on the status of woman – assuming that being takes on anything whatsoever of her destiny. Moreover, it is improper to call her Woman *(la femme)*, because, as I stressed last time, as soon as Woman is enunciated by way of a not-whole, the W cannot be written. There is only barred Woman here.[10] ~~Woman~~ is related to the signifier of A insofar as it is barred. I will illustrate that for you today.

75

---

[7] This might also be rendered, "not being part of it."
[8] It's not clear whether *le* here refers to man or $.
[9] The French is difficult to render with the exact degree of negation: *il n'y a de libido que masculine.*
[10] Same structure as in the preceding footnote: *Il n'y a ici de la que barré.*

The Other is not simply the locus in which truth stammers. It deserves to represent that to which woman is fundamentally related. Assuredly, we have but sporadic testimonies of this, and that is why I took them up last time in their metaphorical function. Being the Other, in the most radical sense, in the sexual relationship, in relation to what can be said of the unconscious, woman is that which has a relationship to that Other. That is what I would like to articulate a little more precisely today.

Woman has a relation to the signifier of that Other, insofar as, qua Other, it can but remain forever Other. I can only assume here that you will recall my statement that there is no Other of the Other. The Other, that is, the locus in which everything that can be articulated on the basis of the signifier comes to be inscribed, is, in its foundation, the Other in the most radical sense. That is why the signifier, with this open parenthesis, marks the Other as barred: S($\cancel{A}$).

How can we conceive of the fact that the Other can be, in some sense *(quelque part)*, that to which half – since that it also roughly the biological proportion – half of all speaking beings refer *(se réfère)?*[11] That is nevertheless what is written on the blackboard with the arrow that begins from ~~Woman~~. ~~Woman~~ cannot be said *(se dire)*. Nothing can be said of woman. Woman has a relation with S($\cancel{A}$), and it is already in that respect that she is doubled, that she is not-whole, since she can also have a relation with Φ.

I designate Φ as the phallus insofar as I indicate that it is the signifier that has no signified, the one that is based, in the case of man, on phallic jouissance. What is the latter if not the following, which the importance of masturbation in our practice highlights sufficiently – the jouissance of the idiot?

2

After that, to calm you back down, I need but speak to you of love – which I will do in a moment. But what does it mean that I have come to such a pass as to speak to you of love, whereas it is not very compatible with the direction from which analytic discourse can provide a semblance of something that would be science?[12]

You are barely aware of this "would be science." Of course, you know, because I have made you take notice of it, that there was a time when one could, not without reason, assure oneself that scientific discourse was grounded in the Galilean turning point. I have stressed that enough to

[11] The French here could also be translated as "refer themselves," "are related," "relate themselves," etc.
[12] The French here, *serait science,* reappears in the next sentence; in both cases it could also be translated as "would like to be science" or "would constitute science."

assume that, at the very least, some of you have gone back to the sources, I mean to Koyré's work.

Regarding scientific discourse, it is very difficult to maintain equally present two terms that I will mention to you.

On the one hand, scientific discourse has engendered all sorts of instruments that we must, from our vantage point here, qualify as gadgets. You are now, infinitely more than you think, subjects of instruments that, from the microscope right down to the radiotelevision, are becoming the elements of your existence. You cannot currently even gauge the import of this, but it is nonetheless part of what I am calling scientific discourse, insofar as a discourse is what determines a form of social link.

On the other hand – and here there is no linkup – there is a subversion of knowledge *(connaissance)*. Prior to that, no knowledge was conceived that did not participate in the fantasy of an inscription of the sexual link. One cannot even say that the subjects of antiquity's theory of knowledge did not realize that.

Let us simply consider the terms "active" and "passive," for example, that dominate everything that was cogitated regarding the relationship between form and matter, a relationship that was so fundamental, and to which each of Plato's steps refers, and then Aristotle's, concerning the nature of things. It is visible and palpable that their statements are based only on a fantasy by which they tried to make up for what can in no way be said *(se dire)*, namely, the sexual relationship.

The strange thing is that in this crude polarity that makes matter passive and form the agent that animates it, something, albeit something ambiguous, nevertheless got through, namely, that this animation is nothing other than the *a* with which the agent animates what? He animates nothing – he takes the other as his soul.[13]

Consider what progresses over the course of the ages regarding the idea of a God that is not the God of Christian faith, but that of Aristotle – the
77   unmoved mover, the supreme sphere. The idea that there is a being such that all other beings with less being than it can have no other aim than being the most being they can be, is the whole foundation of the idea of the Good in Aristotle's ethics, which I encouraged you to look at in order to grasp the impasses therein. If I base myself now on the inscriptions on the blackboard, it is assuredly revealed that it is in the opaque place of jouissance of the Other, of this Other insofar as woman, if she existed, could be it, that the Supreme Being is situated – this Supreme Being that is manifestly mythical in Aristotle's work, this unmoving sphere from which all movements

---

[13] The French, *il prend l'autre pour son âme,* could also be translated as "he (mis)takes the other for his soul."

stem, whatever they may be: changes, generations, motions, translations, increases, etc.

It is insofar as her jouissance is radically Other that woman has more of a relationship to God than anything that could have been said in speculation in antiquity following the pathway of that which is manifestly articulated only as the good of man.

The aim of my teaching, insofar as it pursues what can be said and enunciated on the basis of analytic discourse, is to dissociate *a* and A by reducing the first to what is related to the imaginary and the other to what is related to the symbolic.[14] It is indubitable that the symbolic is the basis of what was made into God. It is certain that the imaginary is based on the reflection of one semblable in another.[15] And yet, *a* has lent itself to be confused with S($\bar{A}$), below which it is written on the blackboard, and it has done so by means of the function of being. It is here that a scission or detachment remains to be effectuated. It is in this respect that psychoanalysis is something other than a psychology. For psychology is this uneffectuated scission.

3

Now, in order to rest a little, I'm going to allow myself to read to you what I wrote to you a while ago, on what? I wrote from the only place where it is possible to speak of love.

Indeed, people have done nothing but speak of love in analytic discourse. How can one help but sense that, with respect to everything that can be articulated now that scientific discourse has been discovered, it is purely and simply a waste of time? What analytic discourse contributes – and perhaps that is, after all, the reason for its emergence at a certain point in scientific discourse – is that to speak of love is in itself a jouissance.

That is assuredly confirmed by the tangible effect that saying whatever

[14] The French, *ce qui est de l'imaginaire* and *ce qui est du symbolique*, could more literally be translated as "what is of the imaginary" and "what is of the symbolic," or as "what is based on the imaginary" and "what is based on the symbolic."
[15] *Semblable* is often translated as "fellow man" or "counterpart," but in Lacan's usage it refers specifically to the mirroring of two imaginary others *(a* and *a')* who *resemble* each other (or at least see themselves in each other). "Fellow man" – corresponding to the French *prochain* – points to man (not woman), the adult (not the child), and suggests fellowship, whereas *semblable* evokes rivalry and jealousy first and foremost in Lacan's work. "Counterpart" suggests parallel hierarchical structures within which the two people take on similar symbolic roles. My "counterpart" could also be someone who serves to complete or complement me, whereas my *semblable* is someone who is indistinguishable from me, competes with me, and usurps my role (this is especially evident in paranoia, where a total confusion of *a* and *a'* may occur). I have thus preferred to revive here the now archaic English "semblable" found, for example, in *Hamlet*, Act V, Scene II, line 124: "his semblable is his mirror; and who else would trace him, his umbrage, nothing more."

[comes to mind] – the very watchword of the analysand's discourse – is what leads to the *Lustprinzip*, what leads to it most directly, without requiring the accession to the higher spheres that constitutes the foundation of Aristotelian ethics.

78   The *Lustprinzip* is, in effect, based only on the coalescence of *a* with S($\cancel{A}$).

A is barred by us, of course. That doesn't mean that it suffices to bar it for nothing to exist thereof. If by S($\cancel{A}$) I designate nothing other than woman's jouissance, it is assuredly because it is with that that I am indicating that God has not yet made his exit.

That is more or less what I wrote for you. What was I, in the end, writing for you? The only thing one can write that is a bit serious – a love letter.

I'm one of those people who doesn't give the psychological presuppositions, thanks to which all of that lasted so long, a good reputation. Still, it is hard to see why the fact of having a soul should be a scandal for thought – if it were true. If it were true, the soul could not be spoken except on the basis of what allows a being – speaking being, to call it by its name – to bear what is intolerable in its world, which assumes that the soul is foreign to it, in other words, phantasmatic. Which considers the soul to be here – in other words, in this world – owing only to its patience and courage in confronting it. That is confirmed by the fact that, up until our time, the soul has never had any other meaning.

It is here that llanguage, llanguage in French must help me out – not, as it sometimes does, by offering me a homonym, like *d'eux* for *deux* or *peut* for *peu,* or this *il peut peu,*[16] which must be there to serve some purpose for us – but simply by allowing me to say that one "souloves" *(âme).*[17] I soulove, you soulove, he souloves. You see here that we can rely only on writing, especially if we include "I so love soulove."[18]

The soul's existence can thus be thrown into question *(mise en cause)* – that's the right term with which to ask whether it's not an effect of love. In effect, as long as the soul souloves the soul *(l'âme âme l'âme),* sex is not involved. Sex doesn't count here. The elaboration from which the soul results is "hommosexual,"[19] as is perfectly legible in history.

What I said earlier about the soul's courage and patience in bearing the world is the true warrant *(répondant)* of what makes Aristotle, in his search for the Good, come up with the following – each of the beings in the world can only orient itself toward the greatest being by confounding its good, its

---

[16] He (or it) can do little.

[17] Lacan here is combining *aimer,* "to love," and *âme,* "soul."

[18] The French, *jamais j'âmais,* literally means "Never did I soulove," which could also be rendered as "Never did I so soulove."

[19] *Hommosexuelle* is a play on *homme,* "man," and "homosexual."

own good, with that with which the Supreme Being shines. What Aristotle evokes with the term φιλία, namely, what represents the possibility of a bond *(lien)* of love between two of these beings, can also, manifesting the tension toward the Supreme Being, be reversed in the way in which I expressed it – it is in their courage in bearing the intolerable relationship to the Supreme Being that friends, φίλοι, recognize and choose each other. This ethics is manifestly "beyondsex" *(hors-sexe)*,[20] so much so that I would like to give it the accent that Maupassant provides by enunciating somewhere in his work the strange term "Horla."[21] The "Beyondsex" *(Horsexe)* is the man about whom the soul speculated.

But it turns out that women too are in soulove *(âmoureuses)*, in other words, that they soulove the soul. What can that soul be that they soulove in their partner, who is nevertheless homo to the hilt, from which they cannot get away? That can only, in effect, lead them to this final term – and it is not for nothing that I call it as I do – ὑστερια, as it is said in Greek, hysteria, namely, to play the part of the man *(faire l'homme)*,[22] as I have said, being thus *hommosexual* or *beyondsex* themselves – it being henceforth difficult for them not to sense the impasse that consists in the fact that they love each other as the same *(elles se mêment)*[23] in the Other, for, indeed, there is no need to know you are Other to be there *(il n'y a pas besoin de se savoir Autre pour en être)*.

So that the soul may come into being, woman is differentiated from it right from the beginning. She is called woman *(on la dit-femme)* and defamed *(dif-fâme)*.[24] The most famous *(fameux)* things that have come down to us about women in history are, strictly speaking, what one can say that is infamous *(infamant)*.[25] It is true that she retains the honor of Cornelia, the mother of the Gracchuses. There's no need to speak of Cornelia to analysts, who hardly ever think of her, but speak to them of any old Cornelia and they'll

---

[20] Or "outside of sex."

[21] Guy de Maupassant's short story, *"Le Horla,"* can be found in the *Oeuvres complètes de Guy de Maupassant* (Paris: Louis Conard, 1927), volume 18, pp. 3–48; in English, see *The Life of Henri René Guy de Maupassant* (New York: M. Walter Dunne, 1903), volume 2, pp. 1–35.

[22] *Faire l'homme* means both "to make the man" (e.g., make a man of him) and "to play the man's part"; both meanings may perhaps be expressed in the English "to constitute a man."

[23] This neologistic expression is based on *elles s'aiment* – "they love themselves or each other" – and *même*, which means same in this context. The expression seems to suggest that they find themselves to be the same (in the Other) and love each other for their similarities or love themselves in each other. The last few words of the sentence, *pour en être*, could also be translated as "to be part of it" or "to participate in it."

[24] *Dit-femme* and *diffâme* are homonyms in French; the latter also contains *âme*, "soul."

[25] *Infamant* also means "defamatory." Phonemically speaking, *fameux* and *infamant* both contain *femme*, "woman."

79

tell you that it won't be very good for her children, the Gracchuses *(Gracques)* – they'll tell whoppers *(craques)* until the end of their existence.

That was the beginning of my letter, an âmusement.

Next I made an allusion to courtly love, which appeared at the time at which hommosexual âmusement had fallen into supreme decadence, in that sort of impossible bad dream known as feudalism. At that level of political degeneracy, it must have become perceptible that, for woman, there was something that could no longer work at all.

The invention of courtly love is not at all the fruit of what people are historically used to symbolizing with the "thesis-antithesis-synthesis." There wasn't the slightest synthesis afterward, of course – in fact, there never is. Courtly love shone as brightly as a meteor in history and afterward we witnessed the return of all the bric-a-brac of a supposed renaissance of stale antiquities. Courtly love has remained enigmatic.

Here there is a little parenthesis – when one gives rise to two *(quand un fait deux)*, there is never a return. They don't revert to making one again, even if it is a new one. *Aufhebung* is one of philosophy's pretty little dreams.

After the meteor of courtly love, what relegated courtly love to its original futility came from an entirely different partition. It required nothing less than scientific discourse, that is, something that owes nothing to the presuppositions of antiquity's soul.

And it is from that alone that psychoanalysis emerged, namely, the object-ivization of the fact that the speaking being still spends time speaking to no avail *(en pure perte)*. He still spends time speaking for a purpose that is among the shortest-lived – the shortest-lived, I say, because it is no more than still *(encore)* underway. In other words, it will continue only as long as it takes for it to finally be resolved – that's what we have coming to us – demographically.

80   That is not at all what will fix man's relationship with women. It is Freud's genius to have seen that. Freud, what a funny name – *Kraft durch Freud*, it's a whole platform! It is the funniest leap in the sacred farce of history. One could, perhaps, while this turning point lasts, have an inkling of something that concerns the Other, insofar as woman deals with it.

I am providing now an essential complement to something that has already been very clearly seen, but that would be clarified by seeing by what pathways it was seen.

What was seen, but only regarding men, is that what they deal with is object *a*, and that the whole realization of the sexual relationship leads to fantasy. It was seen, of course, regarding neurotics. How do neurotics make love? That is the question with which people began. They couldn't help but notice that there was a correlation with the perversions – which supports my *a*, because *a* is what is there as the cause, whatever the said perversion.

What is amusing is that Freud at first attributed the perversions to women – see the *Three Essays on the Theory of Sexuality.* That is truly a confirmation that, when one is a man, one sees in one's partner what one props oneself up on, what one is propped up by narcissistically.

But people had the opportunity after that to notice that the perversions, such as we believe we discern them in neurosis, are not that at all. Neurosis consists in dreaming, not perverse acts. Neurotics have none of the characteristics of perverts. They simply dream of being perverts, which is quite natural, for how else could they attain their partner?

People then began to meet perverts – they're the ones Aristotle didn't want to see at all costs. There is in them a subversion of behavior based on a savoir-faire, which is linked to knowledge *(savoir),* knowledge of the nature of things – there is a direct connection between sexual behavior and its truth, namely, its amorality. Put some soul at the beginning of that – âmorality. . . .

There is a morality – that is the consequence – of sexual behavior. The morality of sexual behavior is what is implicit in *(sous-entendu)* everything that has been said about the Good.

But endlessly saying good things leads to Kant where morality shows its true colors. That is what I felt I needed to lay out in an article, "Kant with Sade" – morality admits that it is Sade.

You can write Sade however you like: either with a capital *S,* to render homage to the poor idiot who gave us interminable writings on that subject – or with a lower-case *s,* for, in the final analysis, that's morality's way of being agreeable, and in old French, that is what that means[26] – or, still better, you can write it as *çade,* since one must, after all, say that morality ends at the level of the id *(ça),* which doesn't go very far. Stated differently, the point is that love is impossible and the sexual relationship drops into the abyss of nonsense, which doesn't in any way diminish the interest we must have in the Other. 81

What we want to know – in what constitutes feminine jouissance insofar as it is not wholly occupied with man, and even insofar, I will say, as it is not, as such, at all occupied with him – what we want to know is the status of the Other's knowledge *(son savoir).*[27]

If the unconscious has taught us anything, it is first of all that somewhere

---

[26] The old French adjective, *sade,* out of use since the sixteenth century, meant "agreeable" (in reference to persons or things).

[27] The French here could mean "her knowledge," but given the fact that woman is not the grammatical subject of the sentence, and given the context of the preceding and subsequent sentences, "its knowledge" seems more likely, referring thus to the Other. In preceding chapters, however, Lacan raised the question of what woman knows of her jouissance; in any case, later in this section he equates the question of her knowledge with the question of the Other's knowledge.

in the Other it knows *(ça sait)*. It knows because it is based precisely on those signifiers with which the subject constitutes himself.

Now that leads to confusion, because it is difficult for whoever souloves not to think that everything in the world knows what it has to do. If Aristotle props up his God with the unmoving sphere on the basis of which everyone must pursue his good, it is because that sphere is supposed to know what is good for it. That is what the break *(faille)* induced by scientific discourse obliges us to do without.

There is no need to know why – we no longer have any need whatsoever for the knowledge Aristotle situates at the origin. In order to explain the effects of gravitation, we don't need to assume the stone knows where it must land. Imputing a soul to animals makes knowing the act par excellence of nothing other than the body – you see that Aristotle wasn't completely off the wall – except that the body is made for an activity, an ἐνέργεια, and that somewhere the entelechy of this body is based on the substance he calls the soul.

Analysis allows for this confusion by restoring the final cause, by making us say that, as concerns everything at least related to speaking beings, reality is like that – in other words, phantasmatic. Is that something that can, in any way whatsoever, satisfy scientific discourse?

There is, according to analytic discourse, an animal that happens to be endowed with the ability to speak *(qui se trouve parlant)* and who, because he inhabits the signifier, is thus a subject of it.[28] Henceforth, everything is played out for him at the level of fantasy, but at the level of a fantasy that can be perfectly disarticulated in a way that accounts for the following – that he knows a lot more about things than he thinks when he acts. But this isn't tantamount to the beginnings of a cosmology.

That is the eternal ambiguity of the term "unconscious." Certainly, the unconscious is presupposed on the basis of the fact that there is, somewhere in the speaking being, something that knows more about things than he does, but this is not an acceptable model of the world. Psychoanalysis, insofar as it derives its very possibility from the discourse of science, is not a cosmology, though it suffices for man to dream for him to see reemerge this immense bric-a-brac, this cluttered storeroom with which he has to make do, which assuredly makes a soul of him, a soul that is occasionally lovable when something is willing to love it.

A woman can, as I said, love in a man only the way in which he faces the knowledge thanks to which *(dont)*[29] he souloves. But, concerning the knowledge thanks to which *(dont)* he is, the question is raised on the basis of the

82

---

[28] Or "is thus subjected to it."

[29] *Dont* is an extremely versatile pronoun that can be translated in many ways: "of which," "by which," "with which," "about which," "whose," etc.

fact that there is something, jouissance, regarding which *(dont)* it is not possible to say whether a woman can say anything about it, whether she can say what she knows about it.

At the end of today's lecture, I have thus arrived, as always, at the edge of what polarized my subject, namely, whether the question of what she knows about it can be raised. That is no different from the question whether the term she gets off on *(dont elle jouit)* beyond all this "playing" *(jouer)* that constitutes her relationship to man – the term I call the Other, signifying it with an A – whether this term knows anything. For it is in this respect that she herself is subjugated *(sujette)* to the Other, just as much as man.

Does the Other know?

There was someone named Empedocles – as if by chance, Freud uses him from time to time like a corkscrew – of whose work we know but three lines, but Aristotle draws the consequences of them very well when he enunciates that, in the end, God was the most ignorant of all beings according to Empedocles, because he knew nothing of hatred. That is what the Christians later transformed into floods of love. Unfortunately, that doesn't fit, because not to know hatred in the least is not to know love in any way either. If God does not know hatred, according to Empedocles, it is clear that he knows less about it than mortals.

The upshot is that one could say that the more a man can believe a woman confuses him with God, in other words, what she enjoys, the less he hates *(haie)*, the less he is *(est)* – both spellings are intended[30] – and since, after all, there is no love without hate, the less he loves.

March 13, 1973

[30] Lacan is playing here on the equivalent pronunciation of *est* and *haie*.

VIII

Knowledge and truth

HATELOVING (L'HAINAMORATION).

KNOWLEDGE ABOUT TRUTH.

CONTINGENCY OF THE PHALLIC FUNCTION.

FREUD'S CHARITY.

GETTING OFF ON KNOWLEDGE.

THE UNCONSCIOUS AND WOMAN.

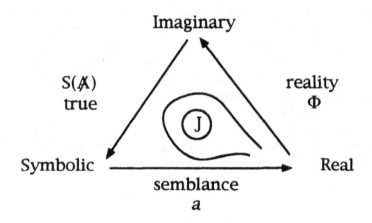

I would really like it if, from time to time, I had a response, even a protest.

I left rather worried the last time, to say the least. It seemed altogether bearable to me, nevertheless, when I reread what I had said – that's my way of saying that it was very good. But I wouldn't be displeased if someone could attest to having understood something. It would be enough for a hand to go up for me to give that hand the floor, so to speak.

I see that no one is putting a hand up, and thus I must go on.

1

What I will willingly write for you today as *"hainamoration"*[1] is the depth *(relief)* psychoanalysis was able to introduce in order to situate the zone of

---

[1] *Hainamoration* is composed of the noun *haine* ("hate") and the adjective *énamoré* ("enamored"). "Depth" probably isn't the best translation for *relief* three words further on; other possible translations include "profile," "terrain," "ground," "outline," and so on.

its experience. It was evidence of good will on its part. If only it had been able to call it by some other name than the bastardized one of "ambivalence," perhaps it would have succeeded better in shaking up the historical setting in which it inserted itself. But perhaps that was modesty on its part.

I mentioned last time that it's no accident Freud arms himself with Empedocles' statement that God must be the most ignorant of all beings, since he does not know hatred. The question of love is thus linked to that of knowledge. I added that Christians transformed God's non-hatred into a mark of love. It is here that analysis reminds us that one knows nothing of love without hate. Well, if the knowledge *(connaissance)* that has been fomented over the course of the centuries disappoints us, and if today we must overhaul the function of knowledge, it is perhaps because hatred has never been put in its proper place.

True, that doesn't seem to be the most desirable thing to mention. That's why I ended last time with the sentence, "One could say that the more a man believes a woman confuses him with God, in other words, what she enjoys," recall the schema I presented last time, "the less he hates," and simultaneously, "the less he is," in other words, in this business, "the less he loves."[2] I wasn't too happy about having ended on that note, which is nevertheless a truth. That is why today I will examine once more in what respect the true and the real apparently get confused.[3]

"The true aims at the real" – that statement is the fruit of a long reduction of pretensions to truth. Wherever truth presents itself, asserts itself as if it were an ideal that could be based on speech,[4] it is not so easily attained. If analysis rests on a presumption, it is that knowledge about truth can be constituted on the basis of its experience.

In the little writing *(gramme)* I gave you of analytic discourse, a is written in the upper left-hand corner, and is supported by S_2, in other words, by knowledge insofar as it is in the place of truth. It is from that point that it[5] interrogates \$, which must lead to the production of S_1, that is, of the signifier by which can be resolved what? Its relation to truth.

$$\frac{a}{S_2} \rightarrow \frac{\$}{S_1}$$

Schema of Analytic Discourse

Truth, let us say, to go right to the quick, is originally ἀλήθεια, a term   85
about which Heidegger speculated extensively. *Emet*, the Hebrew term, is,

---

[2] Lacan has slightly changed his formulation since the last time.
[3] The French here, *se confond*, could also be translated as "overlap."
[4] Or "an ideal of which speech could be the medium (or prop)."
[5] "It" here seems to refer to *a*, but could grammatically refer to S_2 or knowledge.

like every term for truth, of juridical origin. Even in our times, a witness is asked to tell the truth, nothing but the truth, and, what's more, the whole truth, if he can – but how, alas, could he? We demand of him the whole truth about what he knows. But, in fact, what is sought – especially in legal testimony – is that on the basis of which one can judge his jouissance.[6] The goal is that jouissance be avowed, precisely insofar as it may be unavowable. The truth sought is the one that is unavowable with respect to the law that regulates jouissance.

It is also in that sense that, in Kant's terms, the problem is raised of what a free man should do when one proposes to him all the jouissances if he denounces the enemy who the tyrant fears is disputing his jouissance. From the imperative that nothing pathetic[7] should dictate testimony, must we deduce that a free man ought to tell the tyrant the truth, even if that means delivering the enemy or rival into the tyrant's hands by his truthfulness? The reservations sparked in all of us by Kant's answer, which is affirmative, stem from the fact that the whole truth is what cannot be told. It is what can only be told on the condition that one doesn't push it to the edge, that one only half-tells *(mi-dire)* it.

Yet another thing restrains *(ligote)* us regarding the status of truth: the fact that jouissance is a limit. This is related to the very structure that was evoked by my "quadripodes" at the time at which I constructed them for you – jouissance is questioned *(s'interpelle)*, evoked, tracked, and elaborated only on the basis of a semblance.

Love itself, as I stressed last time, is addressed to the semblance. And if it is true that the Other is only reached if it attaches itself *(qu'à s'accoler)*, as I said last time, to *a*, the cause of desire, then love is also addressed to the semblance of being. That there-being[8] is not nothing. It is attributed to *(supposé à)*[9] that object that is *a*.

Shouldn't we find anew here the trace that, insofar as such, it (cor)responds to some imaginary? I have expressly designated that imaginary as *I* (*l'I*), isolated here from the term "imaginary." It is only on the basis of the clothing of the self-image that envelops the object cause of desire that the object relationship[10] is most often sustained – that is the very articulation of analysis.

---

[6] *Ce qu'il en est de sa jouissance* literally means "how things stand with his jouissance," or "the status or state of his jouissance."

[7] "Pathetic" in the Kantian sense of an emotional attachment to a person or thing.

[8] The French here, *cet être-là*, literally "that being over there" or "the being just mentioned," also plays off of the French term for Dasein: *être-là*, "being-there." *Qu'à s'accoler* in the last sentence could also be rendered as "if one attaches oneself."

[9] *Supposé à* would more literally be translated as "assumed in" or "presupposed in."

[10] *Rapport objectal* is not the same as the usual term for object relations in French, *relation d'objet*.

The affinity of *a* to its envelope is one of the major conjunctions put forward by psychoanalysis. To me it essentially introduces a point about which we must be suspicious.

This is where the real distinguishes itself. The real can only be inscribed on the basis of an impasse of formalization. That is why I thought I could provide a model of it using mathematical formalization, inasmuch as it is the most advanced elaboration we have by which to produce signifierness. The mathematical formalization of signifierness runs counter to meaning – I almost said "*à contre-sens*."[11] In our times, philosophers of mathematics say "it means nothing" concerning mathematics, even when they are mathematicians themselves, like Russell.

86

And yet, compared to a philosophy that culminates in Hegel's discourse – a plenitude of contrasts dialectized in the idea of an historical progression, which, it must be said, nothing substantiates for us – can't the formalization of mathematical logic, which is based only on writing *(l'écrit)*, serve us in the analytic process, in that what invisibly holds *(retient)* bodies is designated therein?

If I were allowed to give an image for this, I would easily take that which, in nature, seems to most closely approximate the reduction to the dimensions of the surface writing *(l'écrit)* requires, at which Spinoza himself marveled – the textual work that comes out of the spider's belly, its web. It is a truly miraculous function to see, on the very surface emerging from an opaque point of this strange being, the trace of these writings taking form, in which one can grasp the limits, impasses, and dead ends that show the real acceding to the symbolic.

That is why I do not believe that it was in vain that I eventually came up with the inscriptions *(l'écriture) a*, the $ of the signifier, A, and Φ. Their very writing constitutes a medium *(support)* that goes beyond speech, without going beyond language's actual effects. Its value lies in centering the symbolic, on the condition of knowing how to use it, for what? To retain[12] a congruous truth – not the truth that claims to be whole, but that of the half-telling *(mi-dire)*, the truth that is borne out by guarding against going as far as avowal, which would be the worst, the truth that becomes guarded starting right with *(dès)* the cause of desire.

2

Analysis presumes that desire is inscribed on the basis of a corporal contingency.

[11] *Contre-sens* literally means "counter meaning," "counter direction," "against the tide or current," etc.; figuratively, it means "contradiction."
[12] *Retenir* can mean "to hold," "reserve," "retain," "keep," "carry," "accept," and so on, as well as to "hold back," "check," "stop," "keep back," etc.

Let me remind you what I base this term "contingency" on. The phallus – as analysis takes it up as the pivotal or extreme point of what is enunciated as the cause of desire – analytic experience stops not writing it. It is in this "stops not being written" *(cesse de ne pas s'écrire)*[13] that resides the apex of what I have called contingency.

Analytic experience encounters its terminus *(terme)* here, for the only thing it can produce, according to my writing *(gramme)*, is S_1. I think you still remember the clamor I managed to stir up last time by designating this signifier, S_1, as the signifier of even the most idiotic jouissance – in the two senses of the term, the idiot's jouissance, which certainly functions as a reference here, and also the oddest jouissance.[14]

The necessary is introduced to us by the "doesn't stop" *(ne cesse pas)*. The "doesn't stop" of the necessary is the "doesn't stop being written" *(ne cesse pas de s'écrire)*. Analysis of the reference to the phallus apparently leads us to this necessity.

87   The "doesn't stop not being written," on the contrary, is the impossible, as I define it on the basis of the fact that it cannot in any case be written, and it is with this that I characterize the sexual relationship – the sexual relationship doesn't stop not being written.

Because of this, the apparent necessity of the phallic function turns out to be mere contingency. It is as a mode of the contingent that the phallic function stops not being written. What submits the sexual relationship to being, for speaking beings, but the regime of the encounter is tantamount to contingency. It is only as contingency that, thanks to psychoanalysis, the phallus, reserved in ancient times to the Mysteries, has stopped not being written. Nothing more. It has not entered into the "doesn't stop," that is, into the field on which depend necessity, on the one hand, and impossibility.[15]

The true thus attests here that by making us beware the imaginary, as it does, it has a lot to do with "a-natomy."

It is, in the final analysis, from a depreciatory perspective that I contribute the three terms I write as a, S($\mathbb{A}$), and Φ. They are written on the triangle constituted by the Imaginary, the Symbolic, and the Real.[16]

To the right is the scant reality *(peu-de-réalité)*[17] on which the pleasure

---

[13] *S'écrire* could less idiomatically be translated as "to write itself" or "writing itself."

[14] The Greek root of "idiot," ιδιοτης, means "particular" or "peculiar."

[15] I have left out two words before "impossibility," *plus haut*, which are quite vague and could be rendered as "higher up" or "above that" (as if Lacan were referring to a diagram), or as "before that" or "prior to that."

[16] See the triangle on the first page of this chapter.

[17] Cf. André Breton's use of this term in *"Discours sur le peu de réalité"* in his *Oeuvres complètes* (Paris: Pléaïdes, 1993), vol. 2.

principle is based, which is such that everything we are allowed to approach by way of reality remains rooted in fantasy.

On the other side, what is S($\cancel{A}$) but the impossibility of telling the whole truth *(tout le vrai)*, about which I spoke earlier?

Lastly, the symbolic, directing itself toward the real, shows us the true nature of object *a*. If I qualified it earlier as a semblance of being, it is because it seems to give us the basis *(support)* of being. In everything elaborated on being and even on essence, in Aristotle's work for example, we can see, if we read it on the basis of analytic experience, that object *a* is what is at stake. Contemplation, for example, Aristotelian contemplation, is based on the gaze, as I defined it in *The Four Fundamental Concepts of Psychoanalysis*, as one of the four media *(supports)* that constitute the cause of desire.

With such a "graphicization" – not to say "graph," because that term has a precise meaning in mathematical logic – we see the correspondences that make the real an open [set] between semblance, a result of the symbolic, and reality as it is based on the concreteness of human life: on what leads men, on what makes them always run headlong down the same pathways, and on what is such that the yet-to-be-born *(encore-à-naître)* will never yield anything but *l'encorné.*[18]

On the other side we have *a*. Being on the right path, overall, it would have us take it for being, in the name of the following – that it is apparently something. But it only dissolves *(se résout)*, in the final analysis, owing to its failure, unable, as it is, to sustain itself in approaching the real.

The true, then, of course, is that. Except that it is never reached except by twisted pathways. To appeal to the true, as we are often led to do, is simply to recall that one must not make the mistake of believing that we are already at the level of semblance *(dans le semblant)*. Before the semblance, on which, in effect, everything is based and springs back in fantasy, a strict distinction must be made between the imaginary and the real. It must not be thought that we ourselves in any way serve as a basis for the semblance. We are not even semblance. We are, on occasion, that which can occupy that place, and allow what to reign there? Object *a*.

Indeed, the analyst, of all [those whose] orders of discourse are sustained currently *(actuellement)*[19] – and that word is not nothing, provided we give "action" its full Aristotelian meaning – is the one who, by putting object *a* in the place of semblance, is in the best position to do what should rightfully *(juste)* be done, namely, to investigate the status of truth as knowledge.

88

[18] *L'encorné* is "someone with horns," a reference to someone who has been cheated on: a cuckold. *L'encore-né* ("the reborn") is a homonym.

[19] There is a problem of grammatical structure in this sentence, as Lacan compares the analyst as a person, instead of analytic discourse, to other orders of discourse.

3

What is knowledge? It is strange that, prior to Descartes, the question of knowledge had never been raised. Analysis had to come onto the scene before this question was raised afresh.

Analysis came to announce to us that there is knowledge that is not known, knowledge that is based on the signifier as such. A dream does not introduce us into any kind of unfathomable experience or mystery – it is read in what is said about it, and one can go further by taking up the equivocations therein in the most anagrammatic sense of the word ["equivocations"]. It is regarding that aspect of language that Saussure raised the question whether the strange punctuation marks he found in the saturnine verses were intentional or not.[20] That is where Saussure was awaiting Freud. And it is where the question of knowledge is raised afresh.

If you will excuse me for borrowing from an entirely different register, that of the virtues inaugurated by the Christian religion, there is here a sort of belated effect, an offshoot of charity. Wasn't it charitable of Freud to have allowed the misery of speaking beings to say to itself that there is – since there is the unconscious – something transcendent, truly transcendent, which is but what the species inhabits, namely, language? Wasn't there, yes, charity in the fact of announcing the news that his everyday life has, in language, a more reasonable basis than it seemed before, and that there is already some wisdom – unattainable object of a vain pursuit – there?

Do we need this whole detour to raise the question of knowledge in the form, "What is it that knows?" Do we realize that it is the Other? – such as I posited it at the outset, as a locus in which the signifier is posited, and without which nothing indicates to us that there is a dimension of truth anywhere, a *dit-mension*, the residence of what is said, of this said *(dit)* whose knowledge posits the Other as locus. The status of knowledge implies as such that there already is knowledge, that it is in the Other, and that it is to be acquired *(à prendre)*. That is why it is related to learning *(fait d'apprendre)*.

The subject results from the fact that this knowledge must be learned, and even have a price put on it – in other words, it is its cost that values it, not as exchange but as use. Knowledge is worth just as much as it costs *(coûte)*, a pretty penny *(beau-coût)*,[21] in that it takes elbow grease[22] and that it's difficult. Difficult to what? Less to acquire it than to enjoy it *(d'en jouir)*.

In the enjoying, the conquest of this knowledge is renewed every time it

---

[20] A probable reference to Verlaine's *Poèmes saturniens* (1866).

[21] *Beau-coût* sounds just like *beaucoup* in French.

[22] The French here, *qu'il faille y mettre de sa peau*, could also be translated as "one must pay with one's hide (or skin)" or "one must pay in blood."

is exercised, the power it yields always being directed toward its jouissance.

It is strange that it has never been brought out clearly that the meaning of knowledge resides altogether in the fact that the difficulty of its exercise is the very thing that increases the difficulty of its acquisition. That is because, with every exercise of this acquisition, we find anew that there's no point asking which of these repetitions was the first to have been learned.

Of course there are things that run and that certainly seem to work like little machines – they are called computers. I am willing to accept the notion that a computer thinks. But that it knows, who would say such a thing? For the foundation of knowledge is that the jouissance of its exercise is the same as that of its acquisition.

Here we encounter in a sure manner, surer than in Marx's own work, the true nature of use value, since in Marx's work use value serves only as an ideal point in relation to exchange value, to which everything is reduced.

Let us talk about this learned *(appris)* that is not based on exchange. With Marx's knowledge of politics – which is not nothing – one cannot do "*commarxe,*"[23] if you will allow me. No more than one can, with Freud's knowledge, *defraud.*

One has but to look to see that, wherever one does not come by such knowledge *(ces savoirs)* by pounding it into one's head by tough experience, it falls flat. It can neither be imported nor exported. There is no information that stands up unless it is shaped for use *(formé à l'usage).*

Thus is deduced the fact that knowledge is in the Other and owes nothing to being except that the latter has borne *(véhiculé)* the letter thereof. From whence it results that being can kill where the letter reproduces, but never reproduces the same, never the same being of knowledge.

I think you must have an inkling now of the function I grant the letter in relation to knowledge. I beg you not to too quickly associate this function with so-called messages, for it makes the letter analogous to a germ cell, which, in the realm of molecular physiology, must be strictly separated from the bodies with respect to which it transmits *(véhicule)* life and death together.

Marx and Lenin, Freud and Lacan are not coupled in being. It is via the letter they found in the Other that, as beings of knowledge, they proceed two by two, in a supposed Other. What is new about their knowledge is that it doesn't presume the Other knows anything about it – certainly not the being who constituted the letter there[24] – for it is clearly on the basis of the   90

[23] A combination of commerce and Marx.

[24] The French here, *l'être qui y a fait lettre,* could also be translated as "the being who played the part of (or became) the letter there." The words I have translated as "it doesn't presume the Other knows anything about it," *n'en est pas supposé que l'Autre en sache rien,* could also be translated as "it doesn't presume the Other knows nothing about it."

Other *(de l'Autre)*[25] that he constituted the letter at his own expense, at the price of his being, which, by God, is not nothing at all for each of us, but not a whole lot either, to tell the truth.

I'm going to tell you a little secret about those beings from which the letter is wrought *(d'où se fait la lettre)*. Despite everything people have said, for example, about Lenin, I don't think either hate or love, *hainamoration*, has ever really killed *(étouffé)* anyone. Don't tell me stories about Mrs. Freud! On that score, I have Jung's testimony. He told the truth. Indeed, that was his flaw – he told nothing but that.

Those who still manage to make those kinds of rejections of being are really the ones who partake of scorn *(mépris)*. I will make you write it this time, since today I'm having fun, *méprix*.[26] That makes *uniprix*. We live in the age of supermarkets, so one must know what one is capable of producing, even by way of being.

The hitch is that the Other, the locus, knows nothing. One can no longer hate God if he himself knows nothing – in particular, of what is going on. When one could hate him, one could believe he loved us, since he didn't hate us in return. This is not apparent, despite the fact that, in certain cases, people went at it full speed ahead.

Lastly, as I come to the end of these discourses that I have the strength to pursue before you, I would like to tell you an idea that came to me, about which I have reflected just a little bit. The misfortune of Christ is explained to us by the idea of saving men. I find, rather, that the idea was to save God by giving a little presence and actuality back to that hatred of God regarding which we are, and for good reason, rather indecisive *(mous)*.

That is why I say that the imputation of the unconscious is an incredible act of charity. The subjects know, they know. But all the same, they don't know everything. At the level of this not-everything *(pas-tout)*, only the Other doesn't know. It is the Other who constitutes the not-everything, precisely in that the Other is the part of the not-at-all-knowledgeable *(pas-savant-du-tout)*[27] in the not-everything.

Thus, it may momentarily be convenient to make the Other responsible for this, to which analysis leads in the most avowed manner, though no one realizes it: if libido is only masculine, it is only from where the dear woman

---

[25] Or "from the Other." It is not clear to me what *il* here (rendered by "he") refers to.
[26] *Prix* itself means "price," and thus *méprix* literally means "mispriced." *Uniprix* (in the next sentence) is the name of a French supermarket and literally means "one price" or "united price." "Supermarkets" (in the sentence after that) is in English in the original.
[27] The French here could also be translated as "not-knowledgeable-of-the-whole."

is whole, in other words, from the place from which man sees her, that the dear woman can have an unconscious.

And what does it help her do?[28] It helps her, as everyone knows, make the speaking being, who is reduced here to man, speak, in other words – I don't know if you have noticed this in analytic theory – it helps her exist only as mother. She has unconscious effects, but her unconscious – at the limit point at which she is not responsible for everyone's unconscious, in other words, at the point at which the Other she deals with, the Other with a capital O, works in such a way that she knows nothing, because the Other knows even less, given how difficult it is to even maintain its existence – this unconscious, what can we say of it, if not to sustain with Freud that it doesn't leave her sitting pretty? 91

The last time, I played *(joué)*, as I allow myself to do, on the equivocation, a bit farfetched, between *il hait* (he hates) and *il est* (he is). I enjoy *(jouis)* that equivocation only insofar as I ask whether it is worthy of a pair of scissors. That is precisely what is at stake in castration.

That being as such may provoke hatred cannot be ruled out. Certainly, Aristotle's whole concern was, on the contrary, to conceive of being as that by which beings with less being participate in the highest of beings. And Saint Thomas succeeded in reintroducing that into the Christian tradition – which is not surprising given that, having spread among the Gentiles, the Christian tradition had necessarily been thoroughly shaped thereby, the upshot being that one had but to pull the strings for it to work again. But do people realize that everything in the Jewish tradition goes against that? The dividing line *(coupure)* there does not run from the most perfect to the least perfect. The least perfect there is quite simply what it is, namely, radically imperfect, and one must but obey with the finger and the eye, if I dare express myself thus, he who bears the name Jahve, and several other names to boot. The latter chose his people and one cannot go against that.

Isn't it revealed therein that it is far better to betray him occasionally than to "be-thrate" him *(l'être-haïr)*,[29] the former being what the Jews obviously did not deprive themselves of doing. They couldn't work it out *(en sortir)* any other way.

On the subject of hatred, we're so deadened *(étouffés)* that no one realizes that a hatred, a solid hatred, is addressed to being, to the very being of someone who is not necessarily God.

We remain stuck – and that is why I said that *a* is a semblance of being –

[28] The French, *à quoi ça lui sert*, could also be translated as "what good does it do her" or "what purpose does it serve for her."

[29] Lacan here combines the verbs to be and to hate, but *l'ê tre-haïr* can also be heard as *le trahir*, "to betray him."

at the level – and it is in that respect that analysis, as always, is a little bit lame – of the notion of jealous hatred, the hatred that springs forth from "jealouissance," the hatred that "sprimages forth" *(s'imageaillisse)*[30] from the gaze of the little guy observed by Saint Augustine. Augustine is there as a third party. He observes the little guy and, *pallidus*, the latter pales in observing the *conlactaneum suum* hanging on the nipple. Fortunately, this [jealouissance] is the first substitute jouissance, according to Freud – the desire evoked on the basis of a metonymy that is inscribed on the basis of a presumed demand, addressed to the Other, that is, on the basis of the kernel[31] of what I called *Ding*, in my seminar, *The Ethics of Psychoanalysis*, namely, the Freudian Thing, in other words, the very neighbor *(prochain)* Freud refuses to love beyond certain limits.

The child who is gazed at has it – he has the *a*. Is having the *a* the same as being it? That is the question with which I will leave you today.

March 20, 1973

92   Complement

Beginning of the next class: THE LINGUIST'S POSITION.

I hardly ever talk about what comes out when it is something by me, especially since I generally have to wait so long for it that my interest in it wanes. Nevertheless, it wouldn't be bad for next time if you read something I entitled *"L'Étourdit,"* that begins with the distance there is between the saying *(dire)* and the said *(dit)*.

The fact that being may reside only in what is said *(Qu'il n'y ait d'être que dans le dit)* is a question I'll leave open. It is certain that nothing is said but of being *(il n'y a du dit que de l'être)*, yet that does not imply the inverse. On the contrary, and this is something I have said *(mon dire)*, the unconscious is only on the basis of what is said *(il n'y a de l'inconscient que du dit)*. We can deal with the unconscious only on the basis of what is said, of what is said by the analysand. That is a saying *(dire)*.

How to say it? That is the question. One cannot speak any old which way, and that is the problem of whoever inhabits language, namely, all of us.

---

[30] *S'imageaillisse* contains *s'image* and *jaillisse* and seems to suggest a sort of springing forth from the image.
[31] The French here could be translated in many different ways due to the ambiguity of the thrice repeated *de: le désir évoqué d'une métonymie qui s'inscrit d'une demande supposée, adressée à l'Autre, de ce noyau. . . .* What I have thrice translated as "on the basis of" could be replaced by "from," "by," "of," or "due to." The third *de* could also be understood as linked to *demande*, thus suggesting the translation "a presumed demand, addressed to the Other, for the kernel. . . ." *Noyau* (kernel) could also be translated as "nucleus" or "core."

That is why today – regarding the gap I wanted to express one day by distinguishing what I do here from linguistics, the former being linguistricks – I asked someone, who to my great appreciation was willing to grant my request, to come today to tell you how things stand currently from the linguist's position. No one is better qualified than the person I present to you, Jean-Claude Milner, a linguist.

End of the class: thank-you's.

I don't know what I can do in the quarter of an hour that remains. I will take an ethical notion as my guide. Ethics, as perhaps can be glimpsed by those who heard me speak about it formerly, is closely related to our inhabiting of language, and it is also – as a certain author whom I will mention another time has laid it out – in the realm of gestures. When one inhabits language, there are gestures one makes, greeting *(salutation)* gestures, prostration gestures on occasion, and gestures of admiration when it is a question of another vanishing point *(point de fuite)* – beauty. That implies that things go no further. One makes a gesture and then one conducts oneself like everyone else, namely, like the rest of the riffraff *(canailles)*.

Nevertheless, there are gestures and then there are gestures. The first gesture that is literally dictated to me by this ethical reference must be that of thanking Jean-Claude Milner for what he has told us concerning the present state of the fault line *(faille)* that is opening up in linguistics itself. That justifies perhaps a certain number of behaviors that we perhaps owe – I'm speaking for myself – only to a certain distance we were at from this science on the rise, when it believed that it could become a science. It was truly urgent for us to obtain the information we have just received. Indeed, it is very hard not to realize that, regarding analytic technique, if the subject sitting across from us doesn't say anything, it is a difficulty concerning which the least one can say is that it is altogether unusual *(spéciale)*.   93

What I put forward, by writing *lalangue* [llanguage] as one word, is that by which I distinguish myself from structuralism, insofar as the latter would like to integrate language into semiology – and that seems to me one of the numerous lights Jean-Claude Milner shed on things. As is indicated by the little book that I had you read entitled *The Title of the Letter,* what is at stake in everything I have put forward is the sign's subordination with respect to the signifier.

I must also take the time to render homage to Recanati who, in his intervention, certainly proved to me that I had been heard *(entendu).*[32] This can be seen in all the cutting-edge questions he raised – they are, in a sense, the

---

[32] *Entendu* also means "understood."

questions for which I have the rest of the year to provide you with what I now have by way of a response. The fact that he ended on the question of Kierkegaard and Regine is absolutely exemplary. As I had hitherto made but a brief allusion to them, it was certainly his own contribution. One cannot better illustrate the way in which the ground-breaking I am engaging in before you resonates, than when someone grasps what is at stake. The questions he asked me will certainly be helpful in what I will say to you in what follows. I will ask him for the written text of his talk so that I can refer to it when I am about to respond.

He also referred to Berkeley, and it is insofar as there wasn't the slightest allusion to Berkeley in what I have enunciated before you that I am still more grateful to him. To tell you the whole story, I even took the trouble quite recently to find a first edition – you see I'm a bibliophile, but it's only books I want to read that I try to find first editions of – and thus, last Sunday, I again came across the *Minute Philosopher,* also known as *Alciphron.* It is clear that if Berkeley hadn't been among my earliest reading, many things, including my freewheeling use of linguistic references, probably wouldn't have been possible.

I would nevertheless like to say something concerning the schema Recanati had to erase earlier.[33] To be hysterical or not – that is truly the question. Is there One or not? In other words, this not-whole *(pas-toute),* in classical logic, seems to imply the existence of the One that constitutes *(fait)* an exception. Henceforth, it would be there that we would see the emergence in an abyss – and you will see why I qualify it thusly – of that existence, that at-least-one existence that, with regard to the function Φx, is inscribed in order to speak it *(s'inscrit pour la dire).*[34] For the property of what is said is being, as I said earlier. But the property of the act of saying is to ex-sist in relation to any statement *(dit)* whatsoever.[35]

94

The question then arises whether, given a not-whole, an objection to the universal, something can result that would be enunciated as a particular that contradicts the universal – you can see that I am remaining here at the level of Aristotelian logic.[36]

In that logic, on the basis of the fact that one can write "not-every *(pas-tout)* x is inscribed in Φx," one deduces by way of implication that there is

[33] Recanati apparently spoke at Lacan's seminar four months earlier, and thus it seems there may be an error in the French text here. Recanati had also mentioned Berkeley when he spoke at Lacan's Seminar the year before (June 14, 1972).

[34] *La* here could refer either to "existence" or "function," but "function" seems most likely.

[35] The French here reads *exister,* but the context seems to require *ex-sister.*

[36] As Aristotelian logic is usually understood, $\sim\forall x\Phi x$ (that is, not all x's such that phi of x) would normally imply $\exists x\sim\Phi x$ (that is, the *existence* of a particular x to which the phi function does not apply, of an x that denies universality).

an x that contradicts it. But that is true on one sole condition, which is that, in the whole or the not-whole in question, we are dealing with the finite. Regarding that which is finite, there is not simply an implication but a strict equivalence.[37] It is enough for there to be one that contradicts the universalizing formula for us to have to abolish that formula and transform it into a particular. The not-whole becomes the equivalent of that which, in Aristotelian logic, is enunciated on the basis of the particular. There is an exception. But we could, on the contrary, be dealing with the infinite. Then it is no longer from the perspective of extension that we must take up the not-whole *(pas-toute)*. When I say that woman is not-whole and that that is why I cannot say Woman, it is precisely because I raise the question *(je mets en question)* of a jouissance that, with respect to everything that can be used[38] in the function Φx, is in the realm of the infinite.

Now, as soon as you are dealing with an infinite set, you cannot posit that the not-whole implies the existence of something that is produced on the basis of a negation or contradiction. You can, at a pinch, posit it as an indeterminate existence. But, as we know from the extension of mathematical logic, that mathematical logic which is qualified as intuitionist, to posit a "there exists," one must also be able to construct it, that is, know how to find where that existence is.

I base myself on that when I produce this quartering *(écartèlement)*[39] that posits an existence that Recanati has very well qualified as eccentric to the truth. This indetermination is suspended between $\exists x$ and $\overline{\exists x}$, between an existence that is found by affirming itself and woman insofar as she is not found,[40] which is confirmed by the case of Regine.

In closing, I will tell you something that will constitute, as is my wont, a bit of an enigma. If you reread somewhere something I wrote entitled "The Freudian Thing," you should find therein the following, that there is only one way to be able to write Woman without having to bar it – that is at the level at which woman is truth. And that is why one can only half-speak of her.

The article on which Jean-Claude Milner's exposé was based can be found in his book, Arguments linguistiques, *pages 179–217 (Paris: Seuil, 1973).*

April 10, 1973

[37] In other words, $\sim \forall x \Phi x = \exists x \sim \Phi x$.

[38] If the French here, *se sert*, is changed to the identically pronounced *se serre*, the words "can be used" could read "is encompassed."

[39] The French here means splitting up or quartering (as by horses), and refers no doubt to Lacan's four formulas of sexuation. The last few words of this sentence, *excentrique à la vérité*, could also be translated as "eccentric with respect to the truth."

[40] *Elle ne se trouve pas* can also mean "she does not find herself."

IX

On the Baroque

WHERE IT SPEAKS, IT ENJOYS, AND IT KNOWS NOTHING.

I think of you *(Je pense à vous)*. That does not mean that I conceptualize you *(je vous pense)*.

Perhaps someone here remembers that I once spoke of a language in which one would say, "I love to you" *(j'aime à vous)*,[1] that language modeling itself better than others on the indirect character of that attack called love.

"I think of you" *(Je pense à vous)* already constitutes a clear objection to everything that could be called "human sciences" in a certain conception of science – not the kind of science that has been done for only a few centuries, but the kind that was defined in a certain way with Aristotle. The consequence is that one must wonder, regarding the crux *(principe)* of what analytic discourse has contributed, by what pathways the new science that is ours can proceed.

That implies that I first formulate where we are starting from. We are starting from what analytic discourse provides us, namely, the unconscious. That is why I will first refine for you a few formulations that are a bit tough going concerning where the unconscious stands with respect to traditional science. That will lead me to raise the following question: how is a science still possible after what can be said about the unconscious?

I will announce to you already that, as surprising as it may seem, that will lead me to talk to you today about Christianity.

1

I will begin with my difficult formulations, or at least I assume they must be difficult: "The unconscious is not the fact that being thinks" – though that is implied by what is said thereof in traditional science – "the uncon-

---

[1] See Seminar XIX, February 9, 1972.

scious is the fact that being, by speaking, enjoys, and," I will add, "wants
to know nothing more about it." I will add that that means "know nothing
about it at all."

To immediately show you a card I could have made you wait a little while   96
for – "there's no such thing as a desire to know," that famous *Wissentrieb*
Freud points to somewhere.[2]

Freud contradicts himself there. Everything indicates – that is the meaning of the unconscious – not only that man already knows all he needs
to know, but that this knowledge is utterly and completely limited to that
insufficient jouissance constituted by the fact that he speaks.

You see that that implies a question regarding the status of the actual
science we clearly possess that goes by the name of a physics. In what sense
does this new science concern the real? The problem with the kind of science I qualify as traditional, because it comes to us from Aristotle's thought,
is that it implies that what is thought of *(le pensé)*[3] is in the image of thought,
in other words, that being thinks.

To take an example that is close to home for you, I will state that what
makes what we call "human relations" bearable is not thinking about them.

It is on that point that what is comically called "behaviorism"[4] is ultimately based – behavior, according to behaviorism can be observed in such
a way that it is clarified by its end. People hoped to found human sciences
thereupon, encompassing all behavior, there being no intention of any subject presupposed therein. On the basis of a finality posited as the object of
that behavior, nothing is easier – that object having its own regulation –
than to imagine it in the nervous system.

The hitch is that behaviorism does nothing more than inject therein
everything that has been elaborated philosophically, "Aristotlely," concerning the soul. And thus nothing changes. That is borne out by the fact that
behaviorism has not, to the best of my knowledge, distinguished itself by
any radical change in ethics, in other words, in mental habits, in the *fundamental* habit. Man, being but an object, serves an end. He is founded on
the basis of his final cause – regardless of what we may think, it's still there –
which, in this case, is to live or, more precisely, to survive, in other words,
to postpone death and dominate his rival.

It is clear that the number of thoughts implicit in such a world view, such
a "Weltanschauung" as they say, is utterly incalculable. What is at stake is
the constant equation of thought and that which is thought of.[5]

---

[2] See, for example, SE VII, 194, where it is translated as "instinct for knowledge," and SE X, 245 where it is translated as "epistemophilic instinct."
[3] *Le pensé* (unlike *la pensée*, thought) is "that which is conceptualized."
[4] Whenever Lacan mentions behaviorism here, he uses the English term
instead of the French *comportementalisme*.
[5] That is, of thought and the "reality" thought "thinks" or conceptualizes.

What is clearest about traditional science's way of thinking is what is called its "classicism" – namely, the Aristotelian reign of the class, that is, of the genus and the species, in other words, of the individual considered as specified. It is also the aesthetic that results therefrom, and the ethics that is ordained thereby. I will qualify that ethics in a simple way, an overly simple way that risks making you see red, that's the word for it, but you would be wrong to see too quickly – "thought is on the winning side *(du côté du manche),* and that which is thought of is on the other side," which can be read in the fact that the winner is speech – only speech explains and justifies *(rend raison).*[6]

97 In that sense, behaviorism does not leave behind the classical. It is the said winner *(dit-manche)* – the Sunday *(dimanche)*[7] of life, as Queneau says,[8] not without at the same time revealing therein being as abased.

It's not obvious at first. But what I will point out is that that *Sunday* was read and approved of by someone who, in the history of thought, knew quite a bit, namely, Kojève, and who recognized in it nothing less than absolute knowledge such as it is promised to us by Hegel.

2

As someone recently noticed, I am situated *(je me range)* – who situates me? is it him or is it me? that's a subtlety of llanguage[9] – I am situated essentially on the side of the baroque.

That is a reference point borrowed from the history of art. Since the history of art, just like history and just like art, is something that is related not to the winning side but to the sleeve *(la manche),*[10] in other words, to sleight of hand, I must, before going on, tell you what I mean by that – the subject, "I," being no more active in that "I mean" than in the "I am situated."

And that is what is going to make me delve into the history of Christianity. Weren't you expecting it?

[6] *Du côté du manche* also means "thought has the whiphand (or the upper hand)." *Le manche* literally means "handle," and the expression seems to imply "holding the reins." *Rendre raison* is usually used in the expression *rendre raison de quelque chose à quelqu'un,* "to explain or justify something to someone."
[7] With this neologism, *dit-manche,* Lacan is playing on the identical pronunciation of *dimanche,* "Sunday," and the combination of *dit* ("the said" or "spoken") and *manche,* "the winning side" (which also means "set" in tennis and "handle," as mentioned above).
[8] *Le dimanche de la vie* (literally, "The Sunday of Life") is the title of one of Raymond Queneau's novels.
[9] In French, *je me range,* could equally well mean "I situate myself" or "I am situated" (by someone else).
[10] *La manche* is a rubber (or round), as in the card game of bridge, or a sleeve; *la Manche* is the English Channel.

The baroque is, at the outset, the "storyette"[11] or little tale of Christ. I mean what history recounts about a man. Don't blow a fuse trying to figure it out – he himself designated himself as the Son of Man. That is reported by four texts said to be "evangelical," not so much because they bore good news as because (their authors) were announcers who were good at propagating their sort of news. It can also be understood that way, and that strikes me as more appropriate. They write in such a way that there is not a single fact that cannot be challenged therein – God knows that people naturally ran straight at the muleta. These texts are nonetheless what go right to the heart of truth, the truth as such, up to and including the fact I enunciate, that one can only say it halfway.

That is a simple indication. Their shocking success would imply that I take up these texts and give you lessons on the Gospels. You see what that would lead to.

I would do that to show you that those texts can best be grasped in light of the categories I have tried to isolate in analytic practice, namely, the symbolic, imaginary, and real.

To restrict our attention to the first, I enunciated that truth is the "dit-mension," the "mension" of what is said *(la mension du dit)*.[12]

In this vein, you can't say it any better than the Gospels. You can't speak any better of the truth. That is why they are the Gospels. You can't even bring the dimension of truth into play any better, in other words, push away   98
reality in fantasy *(mieux repousser la réalité dans le fantasme)*.[13]

After all, what followed demonstrated sufficiently – I am leaving behind the texts and will confine my attention to their effect – that this dit-mension stands up. It inundated what we call the world, bringing it back to its filthy truth *(vérité d'immondice)*. It relayed what the Roman, a mason like no other, had founded on the basis of a miraculous, universal balance, including baths of jouissance sufficiently symbolized by those famous thermal baths of which only crumbled bits remain. We can no longer have the slightest idea to what extent, regarding jouissance, that took the cake. Christianity rejected all that to the abjection considered to be the world. It is thus not without an intimate affinity to the problem of the true that Christianity subsists.

That it is the true religion, as it claims, is not an excessive claim, all the more so in that, when the true is examined closely, it's the worst that can be said about it.

[11] The term Lacan uses here, *historiole*, seems to be a neologism.
[12] *Mension* is a neologism, combining the homonyms *mansion* (from the Latin *mansio*, "dwelling," which in French was the term for each part of a theater set in the Middle Ages) and *mention* ("mention," "note," or "honors," as in *cum laude*). It is also the last part of the word "dimension."
[13] Or "back reality into fantasy."

Once one enters into the register of the true, one can no longer exit it. In order to relegate the truth to the lowly status it deserves, one must have entered into analytic discourse. What analytic discourse dislodges[14] puts truth in its place, but does not shake it up. It is reduced, but indispensable. Hence its consolidation, against which nothing can prevail – except what still subsists of the wisdom traditions, though they have not confronted it, Taoism, for example, and other doctrines of salvation in which what is at stake is not truth but the pathway, as the very name "Tao" indicates, and to manage to prolong something that resembles it.

It is true that the storyette of Christ is presented, not as the enterprise of saving men, but as that of saving God. We must recognize that he who took on this enterprise, namely Christ, paid the price – that's the least we can say about it.

We should be surprised that the result seems to satisfy people. The fact that God is indissolubly three is such as to make us prejudge that the count "1-2-3" pre-existed him. One of the two following statements must be true: either he takes into account only the retroactive effect *(l'après-coup)* of Christian revelation, and it is his being that suffers a blow – or the three is prior to him, and it is his unity that takes a hit. Whence it becomes conceivable that God's salvation is precarious and ultimately dependent upon the goodwill of Christians.

What is amusing is obviously – I already told you this, but you didn't catch it – that atheism is tenable only to clerics.[15] It is far more difficult for lay people, whose innocence in that realm remains utter and complete. Recall poor Voltaire. He was a clever, agile, devious, and extraordinarily quick-witted guy, but was altogether worthy of being placed in the umbrella stand[16] across the way known as the Pantheon.

Freud fortunately gave us a necessary interpretation – it doesn't stop *(ne cesse pas)* being written, as I define the necessary – of the murder of the son as founding the religion of grace.[17] He didn't say it quite like that, but he clearly noted that this murder was a mode of negation *(dénégation)* that constitutes a possible form of the avowal of truth.

That is how Freud saves the Father once again. In that respect he imitates Jesus Christ. Modestly, no doubt, since he doesn't pull out all the stops.

99

---

[14] This is, perhaps, a reference to Marie Bonaparte's reductionistic translation of Freud's *Wo Es war, soll Ich werden: Le moi déloge le ça* ("The ego dislodges the id").

[15] The French here, *soutenable que par les clercs,* could also be translated as "bearable only to clerics."

[16] The French here, *vide-poches,* literally refers to a small piece of furniture into which one empties one's pockets. Seminar XX was held in the law school across the square from the Pantheon.

[17] See SE XXI, 136.

But he contributes thereto, playing his little part as a good Jew who was not entirely up-to-date.

There are plenty like that.[18] We must regroup them in order to get them moving. How long will it last?

There is something that I would nevertheless like to get at concerning the essence of Christianity. You're going to have to bust your asses to follow me here.

First I will have to back up a bit.

3

The soul – you have to read Aristotle – is obviously what the winning thought leads to.

It is all the more necessary – that is, it doesn't stop being written – since what the thought in question elaborates are thoughts about *(sur)* the body.

The body should impress you more. In fact, that is what impresses classical science – how can it work like that? A body, yours or any other one besides, a roving body, must suffice unto itself.[19] Something made me think of it, a little syndrome that I saw emerge from my ignorance, and that I was reminded of – if it so happened that one's tears dried up, the eye wouldn't work very well anymore. I call such things miracles of the body. That can be grasped immediately. What if the lachrymal gland didn't cry or drip anymore? You would run into trouble.

On the other hand, the fact is that it snivels, and why the devil does it when, corporally, imaginarily or symbolically, someone steps on your foot? Someone *affects* you – that's what it's called. What relation is there between that sniveling and the fact of parrying the unexpected, in other words, getting the hell out of there *(se barrer)?* That's a vulgar formulation, but it says what it means, because it precisely reconverges with the barred subject *(sujet barré),* some consonance of which you hear therein. Indeed, the subject gets the hell out of there *(se barre),*[20] as I said, and more often than it is his turn to do so.

Observe here simply that there are many advantages to unifying the expression for the symbolic, imaginary, and real – I am saying this to you in parentheses – as Aristotle did, who did not distinguish movement from αλλοίωσις. Change and motion in space were for him – though he didn't

---

[18] It is not at all clear to me what Lacan is referring to in this paragraph. *C'est excessivement répandu* could also be translated as "That's all too common." The only plural noun "them" could refer to in the next sentence seems to be Freud and Voltaire (lay people) or the three that God is, mentioned four paragraphs back.

[19] The French, *il faut que ça se suffise,* could also be translated as "it must be self-sufficient (or self-contained)."

[20] The French here literally means "bars himself."

100

realize it – the fact that the subject gets the hell out of there. Obviously Aristotle didn't have the true categories, but, all the same, he sensed things very well.

In other words, what is important is that all that hang together well enough for the body to subsist, barring any accident, as they say, whether external or internal. Which means that the body is taken for what it presents itself to be, an enclosed body *(un corps fermé).*

Isn't it plain to see that the soul is nothing other than the supposed identicalness *(identité)* of this body to everything people think in order to explain it? In short, the soul is what one thinks regarding the body – on the winning side.

And people are reassured by thinking that the body thinks in the same way. Hence the diversity of explanations. When it is assumed to think secretly, there are secretions. When it is assumed to think concretely, there are concretions. When it is assumed to think information, there are hormones. And still further, it gives itself over *(s'adonne)* to DNA *(ADN)*, to Adonis.

All of that to bring you to the following, which I announced at the beginning regarding the subject of the unconscious – because I don't speak just casually, to waste my breath[21] – it is truly odd that the fact that the structure of thought is based on language is not thrown into question in psychology. The said language – that's the only thing that's new in the term "structure," others do whatever they feel like with it, but what I point out is that – the said language brings with it considerable inertia, which is seen by comparing its functioning to signs that are called mathematical – "mathemes" – solely because they are integrally transmitted. We haven't the slightest idea what they mean, but they are transmitted. Nevertheless, they are not transmitted without the help of language, and that's what makes the whole thing shaky.

If there is something that grounds being, it is assuredly the body. On that score, Aristotle was not mistaken. He sorted out many of them, one by one – see his history of animals. But he doesn't manage, if we read him carefully, to link it to his affirmation – naturally you have never read *De Anima (On the Soul)*, despite my supplications – that man thinks *with* – instrument – his soul, that is, as I just told you, the presumed mechanisms on which the body is based.

Naturally, you have to watch out. We are the ones who introduce mechanisms because of our physics – which is already, moreover, on a dead end path because, ever since the rise of quantum physics, mechanisms don't

---

[21] The French here, *comme on flûte* (literally, "the way people play the flute"), recalls the expression, *c'est comme si je flûtais,* meaning "as if I were talking to a brick wall, to no purpose, to myself," etc.

work. Aristotle didn't enter into the narrow straits of mechanisms. Thus, "man thinks with his soul" means that man thinks with Aristotle's thought. In that sense, thought is naturally on the winning side.

It is obvious that people have nevertheless tried to do better. There is still something else prior to quantum physics – "energetism" and the idea of homeostasis. What I called inertia in the function of language is such that all speech is an energy not yet taken up in an energetics, because that energetics is not easy to measure. Energetics means bringing out, in energy, not quantities, but numbers chosen in a completely arbitrary fashion, with which one arranges things in such a way that there is always a constant somewhere. We are forced to take up the inertia in question at the level of language itself.

What possible relationship can there be between the articulation that constitutes language and the jouissance that reveals itself to be the substance of thought, of that thought so easily reflected in the world by traditional science? That jouissance is the one that makes it such that God is the Supreme Being and that that Supreme Being can, as Aristotle said, be nothing other than the locus in which the good of all the others is known. That doesn't have much to do with thought – does it? – if we consider it to be dominated above all by the inertia of language.

It's not very surprising that no one knew how to grasp or catch jouissance, how to make it squeal, by using what seems to best prop up the inertia of language, namely, the idea of a chain, in other words, bits of string – bits of string that constitute rings and hook onto each other, though we're not too sure how.

I already presented this notion to you once before, and I will try to do better. Last year – I myself am surprised, as I get older, that last year's things seem a hundred years away to me – I took as my theme a formulation that I felt I could base on the Borromean knot: "I ask you to refuse what I offer you because that's not it" *(parce que ce n'est pas ça)*.[22]

That formulation is carefully designed to have an effect, like all those I proffer. See *"L'Étourdit."* I didn't say "the saying remains forgotten" and so on – I said "the fact that one says." Similarly here, I did not say "because that's all it is" *(parce que ce n'est que ça)*.

"That's not it" is the very cry by which the jouissance obtained is distinguished from the jouissance expected. It is here that what can be said in language is specified. Negation certainly seems to derive therefrom. But nothing more.

Structure, which connects up here, demonstrates nothing if not that it is of the same text as jouissance, insofar as, in marking by what distance jouis-

[22] See Seminar XIX, . . . *ou pire,* class given on February 9, 1972.

sance misses – the jouissance that would be in question if "that were it" – structure does not presuppose merely the jouissance that would be it, it also props up another.

Voilà. This dit-mension – I am repeating myself, but we are in a domain where law is repetition – this dit-mension is Freud's saying *(dire)*.

Indeed, that is the proof of Freud's existence – in a certain number of years we will need one. Earlier I associated him with a little friend, Christ. The proof of Christ's existence is obvious: it's Christianity. Christianity, in fact, is attached to it. Anyway, for the time being, we have the *Three Essays on the Theory of Sexuality* that I asked you to look at, because I will have to use it again concerning what I call *la dérive* to translate *Trieb*, the drift of jouissance.[23]

All of that, I insist, is precisely what was covered over *(collabé)* during the whole of philosophical antiquity by the idea of knowledge.

Thank God, Aristotle was intelligent enough to isolate in the intellect-agent what is at stake in the symbolic function. He simply saw that the symbolic is where the intellect must act *(agir)*. But he wasn't intelligent enough – because he hadn't benefited from *(joui de)* Christian revelation – to think that speech *(une parole)*,[24] even his own, by designating the νοῦς that is based only on language, concerns jouissance, the latter nevertheless being designated metaphorically throughout his work.

The whole business of matter and form – what a lot of old claptrap it suggests concerning copulation! It[25] would have allowed him to see that that's not it at all, that there isn't the slightest knowledge *(connaissance)*, but that the jouissances that prop up the semblance thereof are something like the spectrum of white light – on the sole condition that one see that the jouissance at stake is outside the field of that spectrum.

It's a question of metaphor. Regarding the status of jouissance, we must situate the false finality as corresponding to the pure fallacy of a jouissance that would supposedly correspond to the sexual relationship.[26] In this respect, all of the jouissances are but rivals of the finality that would be constituted if jouissance had the slightest relationship with the sexual relationship.

---

[23] *Dérive* literally means "drift," but is very close in spelling to the English term for *Trieb*, "drive."

[24] Or "a word."

[25] "It" here seems to refer back to "Christian revelation" or to the notion that speech concerns jouissance.

[26] The French here, *adéquate au rapport sexuel*, implies a number of things that English cannot adequately render in a word: a jouissance that is supposedly "adequate to the sexual relationship," "sufficient for a sexual relationship (to be constituted)," and "appropriate." It would answer to it or correspond to it.

4

I'm going to add a little more frosting on the Christ, because he is an
important personage, and because it fits into my commentary on the
baroque. It's not without reason that people say that my discourse has
something baroque about it.

I am going to raise a question – of what importance can it be in Christian
doctrine that Christ have a soul? That doctrine speaks only of the incarnation of God in a body, and assumes that the passion suffered in that person
constituted another person's jouissance. But there is nothing lacking here,
especially not a soul.

Christ, even when resurrected from the dead, is valued for his body, and
his body is the means by which communion in his presence is incorpora-
tion – oral drive – with which Christ's wife, the Church as it is called, contents itself very well, having nothing to expect from copulation.

In everything that followed from the effects of Christianity, particularly
in art – and it's in this respect that I coincide with the "baroquism" with
which I accept to be clothed – everything is exhibition of the body evoking
jouissance – and you can lend credence to the testimony of someone who
has just come back from an orgy of churches in Italy – but without copulation. If copulation isn't present, it's no accident. It's just as much out of
place there as it is in human reality, to which it nevertheless provides suste-   103
nance with the fantasies by which that reality is constituted.

Nowhere, in any cultural milieu, has this exclusion been admitted to
more nakedly. I will even go a bit further – don't think I don't mete out
what I say *(mes dires)* to you – I will go so far as to tell you that nowhere
more blatantly than in Christianity does the work of art as such show itself
as what it has always been in all places – obscenity.

The dit-mension of obscenity is that by which Christianity revives the
religion of men. I'm not going to give you a definition of religion, because
there is no more a history of religion than a history of art. "Religions,"
like "the arts," is nothing but a basket category, for there isn't the slightest
homogeneity therein.

But there is something in the utensils people keep fabricating to one-up
each other. What is at stake, for those beings whose nature it is to speak, is
the urgency constituted by the fact that they engage in amorous diversions
(déduits)[27] in ways that are excluded from what I could call "the soul of
copulation," were it conceivable, in the sense that I gave earlier to the word
"soul," namely, what is such that it functions. I dare to prop up with this
word that which – effectively pushing them to it if it were the soul of copula-

[27] *Déduits amoureux* could also be translated as "amorous pursuits."

tion – could be elaborated by what I call a physics, which in this case is nothing other than the following: a thought that can be presupposed in thinking.[28]

There is a hole there and that hole is called the Other. At least that is what I felt I could name *(dénommer)* it, the Other qua locus in which speech, being deposited *(déposée)*[29] – pay attention to the resonances here – founds truth and, with it, the pact that makes up for the non-existence of the sexual relationship, insofar as it would be conceptualized *(pensé)*, in other words, something that could conceivably be conceptualized *(pensé pensable)*,[30] and that discourse would not be reduced to beginning solely from semblance – if you remember the title of one of my seminars.[31]

The fact that thought moves in the direction of a science[32] only by being attributed to thinking[33] – in other words, the fact that being is presumed to think – is what founds the philosophical tradition starting from Parmenides. Parmenides was wrong and Heraclitus was right. That is clinched by the fact that, in fragment 93, Heraclitus enunciates οὔτε λέγει οὔτε κρύπτει ἀλλὰ σημαίνει, "he neither avows nor hides, he signifies" – putting back in its place the discourse of the winning side itself – ὁ ἄναξ οὗ τὸ μαντεῖόν ἐστι τὸ ἐν Δελφοῖς, "the prince" – in other words, the winner – "who prophecizes in Delphi."[34]

You know the crazy story, the one that arouses my delirious admiration? I roll on the floor laughing when I read Saint Thomas (Aquinas), because it's awfully well put together. For Aristotle's philosophy to have been reinjected by Saint Thomas into what one might call the Christian conscience, if that had any meaning, is something that can only be explained by the fact that Christians – well, it's the same with psychoanalysts – abhor what was revealed to them. And they are right.

104   The gap inscribed in the very status of jouissance qua dit-mension of the

[28] The French here, *une pensée supposable au penser,* could also be translated as "a thought attributable to thinking."

[29] *Déposée* also means registered (as in a *marque déposée,* "a registered trademark") and deposed (as when a monarch is stripped of power).

[30] The awkwardness of this formulation is based on the fact that Lacan shifts from a verb form, *pensé* (thought of, conceived of, or conceptualized) in *il serait pensé,* to a noun form, *pensé* (what is thought of or conceptualized) in *pensé pensable,* which could perhaps also be rendered as "thinkable matter for thought."

[31] Seminar XVIII was entitled, *D'un discours qui ne serait pas du semblant* ("On a Discourse That Would Not Be Based on Semblance").

[32] *Que la pensée n'agisse dans le sens d'une science* could also be translated as "The fact that thought acts in the sense of a science" or "stirs only in the direction of a science."

[33] Or "presupposed in thinking."

[34] This fragment is number 247 in *The Presocratic Philosophers* by Kirk and Raven (Cambridge: Cambridge University Press, 1957); the authors give ἐστι where the original French text of the Seminar has ἐστλ; the English translation they provide is: "The Lord whose oracle is in Delphi neither speaks out nor conceals, but gives a sign" (211).

body, in the speaking being, is what re-emerges with Freud – and I'm not saying anything more than him – through the test constituted by the existence of speech. Where it speaks, it enjoys *(Là où ça parle, ça jouit)*. And that doesn't mean that it knows anything because, as far as I've heard, the unconscious has revealed nothing to us about the physiology of the nervous system, the process of getting a hard-on, or early ejaculation.

To once and for all put an end to this business about the true religion, I will, while there is still time, point out that God is manifested only in writings that are said to be sacred. Sacred in what respect? In that they don't stop repeating the failure – read Salomon, the master of masters, the master of feeling *(senti-maître)*,[35] someone of my own ilk – the failure of the attempts made by a wisdom tradition to which being is supposed to testify.

None of that implies that there weren't things from time to time thanks to which jouissance – without it, there could be no wisdom – could believe that it had reached the goal of satisfying the thought of being *(la pensée de l'être)*. But that goal has never been satisfied, except at the price of a castration.

In Taoism, for example – you don't know what it is, very few do, but I have worked at it, by reading the texts, of course – this is clear in the very practice of sex. In order to feel good, one must withhold one's cum. Buddhism is the trivial example by its renunciation of thought itself. What is best in Buddhism is Zen, and Zen consists in answering you by barking, my little friend. That is what is best when one wants, naturally, to get out of this infernal business, as Freud called it.

The fantasizing *(fabulation)* of antiquity, mythology as you call it – Claude Lévi-Strauss also called it by that name – of the Mediterranean region – which is precisely the one we don't touch because it's the most profuse and, above all, because such a big to-do has been made of it that one no longer knows by what strand to approach it – mythology has also come to something in the form of psychoanalysis.

There were shovelfuls of gods – all one had to do was find the right one. Which led to this contingent thing that is such that sometimes, after an analysis, we manage to achieve a state in which a guy correctly fucks his "one gal" *(un chacun baise convenablement sa une chacune)*.[36] They were gods

---

[35] *Senti-maître* is a neologism that combines "master" *(maître)* and "sentimental" or "feeling" *(sentir* is "to feel"), and is also a homonym for *centimètre* ("centimeter").

[36] Lacan is modifying a well-known French expression, *À chacun sa chacune,* loosely translated, "A gal for every guy" or "Every guy has his gal." He inserts *un* before *chacun* and *une* after *sa* (rendering it grammatically incorrect) and before *chacune*. The *une chacune* is perhaps Lacan's way of insisting that women cannot be taken as a whole or set (that is, as Woman), but only one by one. A similar expression is found in Seminar XIX (May 4, 1972).

all the same, that is, rather consistent representations of the Other. Let us pass over here the weakness of the analytic operation.

Oddly enough, that is so completely compatible with Christian belief that we saw a renaissance of polytheism during the era known by the same name.

I am telling you all that precisely because I just got back from the museums, and because the Counter-Reformation was ultimately a return to the sources and the baroque the parading thereof.

105   The baroque is the regulating of the soul by corporal radioscopy.

I should sometime – I don't know if I'll ever have the time – speak of music, in the margins. For the time being, I am only speaking of what we see in all the churches in Europe, everything attached to the walls, everything that is crumbling, everything that delights, everything that is delirious.[37] It's what I earlier called obscenity – but exalted.

I wonder what effect this flood of representations of martyrs must have on someone who comes from backwoods China. That formulation can be reversed – those representations are themselves martyrs. You know that "martyr" means witness – of a more or less pure suffering. That was what our painting was about, until the slate was wiped clean when people began to seriously concern themselves with little squares.

There is a reduction of the human species here – that word, "human" *(humaine)*, resounds like "unhealthy humor" *(humeur malsaine)*, and there is a remainder that creates "misfortune" *(malheur)*. That reduction is the term by which the Church intends to carry the species – that's the word for it – right up to the end of time. And it is so well grounded in the gap peculiar to the sexuality of speaking beings that it risks being at least as well grounded, let's say – because I don't want to give up on anything – as the future of science.

The Future of Science is the title of a book by that other priestling named Ernest Renan, who was also an all-out servant of the truth.[38] He only required one thing of truth – but it was absolutely capital, failing which, he panicked – that it have no consequence whatsoever.

The economy of jouissance is something we can't yet put our fingertips on. It would be of some interest if we managed to do so *(qu'on y arrive)*. What we can see on the basis of analytic discourse is that we may have a slight chance of finding out something about it, from time to time, by pathways that are essentially contingent.

---

[37] *Délirer* literally means "to have delusions," "to be delirious," or "to imagine things." Figuratively it means "to go nuts," "to proliferate like mad," and so on.
[38] Renan's book was written in 1848–1849 and finally published in French in 1890 by Calmann-Lévy. It was translated into English by Albert Vandam and C. B. Pitman (London: Chapman, 1891).

If my discourse today hadn't been absolutely and entirely negative, I would tremble at having lapsed into philosophical discourse. Nevertheless, since we have already seen several wisdom traditions that have lasted quite a while, why shouldn't we find, with analytic discourse, something that gives us a glimpse of something precise? After all, what is energetics if it is not also a mathematical thing *(truc)?*[39] The analytic thing will not be mathematical. That is why the discourse of analysis differs from scientific discourse.

Well, let us leave that chance to lady luck – *encore.*[40]

May 8, 1973

[39] *Truc* can also mean "gizmo," "thingamabob," etc.
[40] Lacan transforms the usual expression here, *au petit bonheur la chance,* used when you try to get or do something haphazardly – you leave it to lady luck. He says, *Enfin, cette chance, mettons-la sous le signe d'au petit bonheur – encore.*

X

Rings of string

I dreamt last night that when I arrived, no one was here.

That confirms the wishful character of the dream. Despite the fact that I was rather outraged, that it would all be for naught, since I also remembered in the dream that I had worked until 4:30 in the morning, it was nevertheless the satisfaction of a wish, namely, that then I would have but to twiddle my thumbs.

1

I am going to say – that is my function – I am going to say once again – because I repeat myself – something that I say *(ce qui est de mon dire)*, which is enunciated as follows, "There's no such thing as a metalanguage."

When I say that, it apparently means – no language of being. But is there being? As I pointed out last time, what I say is what there isn't. Being is, as they say, and nonbeing is not. There is or there isn't. Being is merely presumed in certain words – "individual," for instance, and "substance." In my view, it is but a fact of what is said *(un fait de dit)*.[1]

The word "subject" that I use thus takes on a different import.

I distinguish myself from the language of being. That implies that there may be verbal fiction *(fiction de mot)* – I mean, fiction on the basis of the word. And as some of you may recall, that is what I began with when I spoke of ethics.[2]

Just because I have written things that serve the function of forms of language doesn't mean I assure the being of metalanguage. For I would have to present that being as subsisting by itself, all alone, like the language of being.

[1] Or "a spoken fact."
[2] Lacan is referring here to Jeremy Bentham's *Theory of Fictions* (the first chapter of which is entitled "Linguistic Fictions"), mentioned in Seminar VII, *The Ethics of Psychoanalysis*.

Mathematical formalization is our goal, our ideal. Why? Because it alone is matheme, in other words, it alone is capable of being integrally transmitted. Mathematical formalization consists of what is written, but it only subsists if I employ, in presenting it, the language *(langue)* I make use of. Therein lies the objection: no formalization of language is transmissible without the use of language itself. It is in the very act of speaking that I make this formalization, this ideal metalanguage, ex-sist. It is in this respect that the symbolic cannot be confused with being – far from it. Rather, it subsists qua ex-sistence with respect to the act of speaking *(ex-sistence du dire)*. That is what I stressed, in my text called *"L'Étourdit,"* by saying that the symbolic bears only ex-sistence.

In what respect? This is one of the essential things I said last time – analysis can be distinguished from everything that was produced by discourse prior to analysis by the fact that it enunciates the following, which is the very backbone of my teaching – I speak without knowing it. I speak with my body and I do so unbeknownst to myself. Thus I always say more than I know *(plus que je n'en sais)*.

This is where I arrive at the meaning of the word "subject" in analytic discourse. What speaks without knowing it makes me "I," subject of the verb. That doesn't suffice to bring me into being. That has nothing to do with what I am forced to put in being *(mettre dans l'être)* – enough knowledge for it to hold up, but not one drop more.

That is what was hitherto called form. In Plato's work, form is the knowledge that fills being. Form doesn't know any more about it than it says. It is real in the sense that it holds being in its glass, but it is filled right to the brim. Form is the knowledge of being. The discourse of being presumes that being is, and that is what holds it.

There is some relationship of being that cannot be known. It is that relationship whose structure I investigate in my teaching, insofar as that knowledge – which, as I just said, is impossible – is prohibited *(interdit)* thereby. This is where I play on an equivocation – that impossible knowledge is censored or forbidden, but it isn't if you write "inter-dit"[3] appropriately – it is said between the words, between the lines. We have to expose the kind of real to which it grants us access.

We have to show where the shaping *(mise en forme)*[4] of that metalanguage – which is not, and which I make ex-sist – is going. Something true can still be said about what cannot be demonstrated.[5] It is thus that is

---

[3] *Interdit,* in French, means "prohibited" or "forbidden," and is sometimes rendered in English as "interdicted."
[4] The French here usually means "formatting" or "editing," and also includes the Platonic "form."
[5] This is a reference to Gödel's Incompleteness Theorem.

opened up that sort of truth, the only truth that is accessible to us and that bears on, for example, the non-savoir-faire.

I don't know how to approach, why not say it, the truth – no more than woman. I have said that the one and the other are the same thing, at least to man. They constitute the same conundrum *(embarras)*. As it turns out, I relish the one and the other, despite what people say.

109   The discordance between knowledge and being is my subject. One can also say, notwithstanding, that there isn't any discordance regarding what still *(encore)* – according to my title this year – directs the game. We are still *(encore)* caught up in the insufficiency of knowledge. It is what directs the game of encore – not that by knowing more about it, it would direct us better, but perhaps there would be better jouissance, agreement between jouissance and its end.

Now, the end of jouissance – as everything Freud articulates about what he unadvisedly calls "partial drives" teaches us – the end of jouissance does not coincide with *(est à côté de)* what it leads to, namely, the fact that we reproduce.

The "I" is not a being, but rather something attributed to[6] that which speaks. That which speaks deals only with solitude, regarding the aspect of the relationship I can only define by saying, as I have, that it cannot be written. That solitude, as a break in knowledge, not only can be written but it is that which is written *par excellence,* for it is that which leaves a trace of a break in being.

That is what I said in a text, certainly not without its imperfections, that I called *"Lituraterre."*[7] "The cloud of language," I expressed myself metaphorically, "constitutes writing." Who knows whether the fact that we can read *(lire)* the streams I saw over Siberia as the metaphorical trace of writing isn't linked *(lié)* – beware, *lier* (to link) and *lire* consist of the same letters – to something that goes beyond the effect of rain, which animals have no chance of reading as such? It seems rather to be linked to that form of idealism that I would like you to get into your heads – certainly not that professed by Berkeley, who lived at a time when the subject had acquired its independence, not the idealism that holds that everything we know is representation, but rather that idealism related to the impossibility of inscribing the sexual relationship between two bodies of different sexes.

An opening, by which it is the world that makes us into its partner, is created thereby. It is the speaking body insofar as it can only manage to reproduce thanks to a misunderstanding regarding its jouissance. That is to

    [6] Or "presumed in."
    [7] *"Lituraterre"* originally came out in *Littérature* 3 (1971), a French journal published by Larousse. It was reprinted in *Ornicar?* 41 (1987), pp. 5–13.

say that it only reproduces thanks to missing[8] what it wants to say, for what it wants to say *(veut dire)* – namely, as French clearly states, its meaning *(sens)*[9] – is its effective jouissance. And it is by missing that jouissance that it reproduces – in other words, by fucking.

That is precisely what it doesn't want to do, in the final analysis. The proof is that when one leaves it all alone, it sublimates with all its might, it sees Beauty and the Good – not to mention Truth, and it is there, as I just told you, that it comes closest to what is at stake. But what is true is that the partner of the opposite sex *(l'autre sexe)* remains the Other. It is thus by missing its jouissance that it manages to be reproduced yet again *(encore)* without knowing anything about what reproduces it. And in particular – and this is perfectly tangible in Freud's work, though of course it's nothing but gibberish, even if we can't do any better – it doesn't know whether what reproduces it is life or death.

I must nevertheless say what there is qua metalanguage, and in what respect it coincides with the trace left by language. For this is where the subject returns to the revelation of the correlate of language *(langue)*, which is the extra knowledge of being,[10] and constitutes for him his slim chance of going to the Other, to its being, about which I noted last time – and this is the second essential point – that it wants to know nothing. It is a passion for ignorance.

That is why the other two passions are those that are called love – which has nothing to do with knowledge, despite philosophy's absurd contentions – and hatred, which is what comes closest to being, that I call "ex-sisting." Nothing concentrates more hatred than that act of saying in which ex-sistence is situated.

Writing is thus a trace in which an effect of language can be read *(se lit)*. That is what happens when you scribble something.

I certainly don't deprive myself of doing so, for that is how I prepare what I have to say. It is worth noting that one must ensure things by writing *(de l'écriture, s'assurer)*.[11] The latter certainly is not metalanguage, nevertheless,

[8] *Ratage* means "missing," "failing," "backfiring," "misfiring," "messing up," "botching up," "spoiling," and "flunking," as well as "scratching out," "crossing out," etc.
[9] *Sens* also means "sense" and "direction"; it is pronounced exactly like the last syllable in *jouissance*. *Veut dire* literally means "wants to say" but is usually translated as "means." "Effective" here (as elsewhere) could also be rendered as "actual."
[10] The French here, *ce savoir en plus de l'être*, could also be translated as "being's extra knowledge."
[11] The French here could be understood in a number of different ways: "check over writing" or "capture or keep an eye on writing" is what the grammar would dictate, but Lacan's eccentric use of *de* suggests "assure oneself of things by using writing (or by writing things down)."

110

though one can make it fulfill a function that resembles it. That effect is nevertheless secondary with respect to the Other in which language is inscribed as truth. For nothing I could write on the blackboard for you based on the general formulas that relate energy and matter, at the present point in time – Einstein's last formulas, for example – none of it would stand up if I didn't prop it up with an act of speaking that involves language *(langue),* and with a practice which is that of people who give orders in the name of a certain knowledge.

But let me back up. When you scribble and when I too scribble, it is always on a page with lines, and we are thus immediately enmeshed in this business of dimensions.

2

What cuts a line is a point. Since a point has zero dimensions, a line is defined as having one dimension. Since what a line cuts is a surface, a surface is defined as having two dimensions. Since what a surface cuts is space, space has three dimensions.

The little sign I wrote on the blackboard (figure 1) derives its value therefrom.

It has all the characteristics of writing – it could be a letter. However, since you write cursively, you never think of stopping a line before it crosses another in order to make it pass underneath, or rather in order to assume that it passes underneath, because in writing something completely different than three-dimensional space is involved.

111

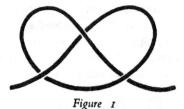

Figure 1

In this figure, when a line is cut by another, it means that the former passes under the latter. That is what happens here, except that there is only one line. But although there is only one, it is distinguished from a simple ring, for this writing represents for you the flattening out *(mise-à-plat)* of a knot. Thus, this line or string is something other than the line I defined earlier with respect to space as a cut and that constitutes a hole, that is, separates an inside from an outside.

This new line is not so easily incarnated in space. The proof is that the ideal string, the simplest string, would be a torus. And it took a long time for people to realize, thanks to topology, that what is enclosed in a torus has absolutely nothing to do with what is enclosed in a bubble.

Regardless of what you do with the surface of a torus, you cannot make a knot. But, on the contrary, with the locus of a torus, as this shows you, you can make a knot. It is in this respect, allow me to tell you, that the torus is reason, since it is what allows for knots.

It is in that respect that what I am showing you now, a twisted torus, is as neat *(sec)* an image as I can give you of the trinity, as I qualified it the other day – one and three in a single stroke.[12]

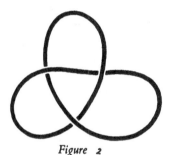

Figure 2

Nevertheless, it is by making three toruses out of it, using a little thinga-mabob I already showed you called the Borromean knot, that we shall be able to operate on the first knot. Naturally, there are people here today who weren't here last year in February when I spoke about the Borromean knot.[13] I will try today to give you a sense of its importance and of how it is related to writing, inasmuch as I have defined writing as what language leaves by way of a trace.   112

With the Borromean knot, we are dealing with something that cannot be found anywhere, namely, a true ring of string. You should realize that, when you lay out a string, you never manage to join the two ends together in the woof *(trame)*. In order to have a ring of string, you have to make a knot, preferably a sailor's knot. Let's make a sailor's knot with this string.

That's it. Thanks to the sailor's knot, we have here, as you see, a ring of string. I will make two more. The problem that is then raised by the Borro-

---

[12] The overhand knot depicted in figure 2 is often referred to in English as a "clover-leaf knot." See *Introduction to Knot Theory* by Richard H. Crowell and Ralph H. Fox (New York: Blaisdell, 1963), 4.

[13] See Seminar XIX, . . . *ou pire,* class given on February 9, 1972.

mean knot is the following – once you have made your rings of string, how can you get these three rings of string to hang together in such a way that if you cut one, all three are set free?

Three is really nothing. The true problem, the general problem, is to work things out in such a way that, with any number of rings of string, when you cut one, every single one of the others becomes free and independent.

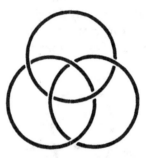

Figure 3

Here is the Borromean knot – I already put it up on the blackboard last year. It is easy for you to see that no two rings of string are knotted to each other, and that it's only thanks to the third that they hang together.

Pay close attention here – don't let yourself remain captivated by this image. I'm going to show you another way to solve the problem.

Here is a ring of string. Here is another. You insert the second ring into the first, and you bend it (see figure 4).

It suffices then to take up the second ring in a third for the three to be knotted together – knotted in such a way that it suffices for you to cut one for the other two to be set free (see figure 5).

Figure 4

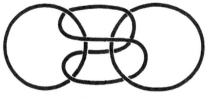

Figure 5

After the first bending, you could also bend the third ring and take it up in a fourth. With four, as with three, it suffices to cut one of the rings[14] for all the others to be set free. You can add an absolutely infinite number of rings and it will still be true. The solution is thus absolutely general, and the line of rings can be as long as you like.

In this chain, whatever its length, the first and last links differ from the others: while the intermediary rings, in other words, the bent ones, are all ear-shaped, as you see in figure 4, the extremes are simple rings.

Nothing stops us from making the first and last rings coincide, by bending the first and taking it up in the last. The chain is thereby closed (see figure 6).

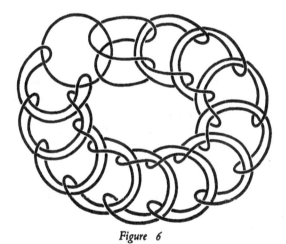

Figure 6

The collapse *(résorption)* of the two extremes into one nevertheless leaves a trace: in the chain of intermediary links, the strands are juxtaposed two

---

[14] The French here reads *noeuds*, "knots," which seems erroneous.

by two, whereas, when the chain closes on a simple, single ring, four strands on each side are juxtaposed to one strand, the circular ring.

That trace can certainly be effaced – you then obtain a homogeneous chain of bent rings.

3

Why did I formerly bring in the Borromean knot? It was to translate the formulation "I ask you" – what? – "to refuse" – what? – "what I offer you" – why? – "because that's not it." You know what "it" is; it's object *a*. Object *a* is no being. Object *a* is the void presupposed by a demand, and it is only by situating demand via metonymy, that is, by the pure continuity assured from the beginning to the end of a sentence, that we can imagine a desire that is based on no being – a desire without any other substance than that assured by knots themselves.

Enunciating that sentence, "I ask you to refuse what I offer you," I could only motivate it by the "that's not it" that I took up again last time.

"That's not it" means that, in the desire of every demand, there is but the request for object *a,* for the object that could satisfy jouissance. The latter would then be the *Lustbefriedigung* presupposed in what is improperly called the "genital drive" in psychoanalytic discourse, that drive[15] in which the full, inscribable relationship of the one with what remains irreducibly the Other is supposedly inscribed. I stressed the fact that the partner of this "I" that is the subject, the subject of any sentence that constitutes a demand, is not the Other, but that which is substituted for it in the form of the cause of desire – that I have diversified into four causes, insofar as the cause is constituted diversely, according to the Freudian discovery, on the basis of the object of sucking, the object of excretion, the gaze, and the voice. It is as substitutes for the Other that these objects are laid claim to[16] and made into the cause of desire.

It seems that the subject calls *(se représente)*[17] inanimate objects to mind as a function of the following – that there's no such thing as a sexual relation. It's only speaking bodies, as I said, that come up with an idea of the world as such. The world, the world of being, full of knowledge, is but a dream, a dream of the body insofar as it speaks, for there's no such thing as a knowing subject *(il n'y a pas de sujet connaissant)*. There are subjects who give themselves correlates in object *a,* correlates of enjoying speech qua

---

[15] The French here, *celle,* could also possibly refer to "jouissance" or *"Lustbefriedigung."*
[16] The French here, *réclamés,* could also be translated as "clamored for" or even "requisitioned."
[17] *Se représenter* literally means "to represent to oneself," and figuratively means "to think, imagine, conceive in one's mind," etc.

jouissance of speech *(parole jouissante en tant que jouissance de parole)*. What does it wedge *(coince-t-elle)*[18] but other Ones?

I pointed out to you earlier that bilobulation – the transformation by bending of the ring of string into two ears – can be carried out in a strictly symmetrical fashion. Indeed, that is what happens as soon as one gets to the level of four. Well, similarly, the reciprocity between the subject and object *a* is total.

For every speaking being, the cause of its desire is, in terms of structure, strictly equivalent, so to speak, to its bending, that is, to what I have called its division as subject. That is what explains why the subject could believe for so long that the world knew as much about things as he did. The world is symmetrical to the subject – the world of what I last time called thought is the equivalent, the mirror image, of thought. That is why there was nothing but fantasy regarding knowledge until the advent of the most modern science.   115

This mirroring is what allowed for the chain[19] of beings that presupposed in one being, said to be the Supreme Being, the good of all beings. Which is also equivalent to the following, that object *a* can be said to be, as its name indicates, a-sexual *(a-sexué)*. The Other presents itself to the subject only in an *a*-sexual form. Everything that has been the prop, substitute-prop, or substitute for the Other in the form of the object of desire is *a*-sexual.

It is in that sense that the Other as such remains a problem in Freudian theory – though we are able to take it a step further – a problem that is expressed in a question Freud repeated – "What does a woman want?" – woman being, in this case, equivalent to truth. It is in that sense that the equivalence I produced is justified.

Does that enlighten you as to why it is of interest to work with the ring of string? The said ring is certainly the most eminent representation of the One, in the sense that it encloses but a hole. Indeed, that is what makes a true ring of string very difficult to produce. The ring of string I make use of is mythical, since people don't manufacture closed rings of string.

But still, what are we to do with this Borromean knot? My answer to you is that it can serve us by representing a metaphor that is so often used to express what distinguishes the use of language – the chain metaphor.

Let us note that, unlike rings of string, the elements of a chain can be forged. It is not very difficult to imagine how – one bends metal to the point where one can solder it. No doubt, it's not a simple prop, for, in order to

---

[18] *Elle* could refer either to speech or jouissance here. On wedging, see the section entitled "Answers" at the end of this chapter. "Wedge" here could also be replaced by "grab hold of" or "corner."

[19] The (great) chain of being, as it is known in English, doesn't include the word "chain" in French: *échelle* means "ladder" or "scale."

be able to adequately represent the use of language, links would have to be made in that chain that would attach to another link a little further on, with two or three floating intermediate links. We would also have to understand why a sentence has a limited duration. The metaphor cannot tell us that.

Do you want an example that can show you what purpose can be served by this line of folded knots that become independent once again as soon as you cut one of them? It's not very difficult to find such an example in psychosis, and that's no accident. Recall what hallucinatorily fills up Schreber's solitude: *"Nun will Ich mich . . .,"* "Now I shall . . .," or again *"Sie sollen nämlich . . .,"* "You were to. . . ."[20] These interrupted sentences, which I called code messages,[21] leave some sort of substance in abeyance. We perceive here the requirement of a sentence, whatever it may be, which is such that one of its links, when missing, sets all the others free, that is, withdraws from them the One.[22]

116   Isn't that the best basis we can provide for that by which mathematical language proceeds?

The nature of mathematical language, once it is sufficiently isolated in terms of its requirements of pure demonstration, is such that everything that is put forward there – not so much in the spoken commentary as in the very handling of letters – assumes that if one of the letters doesn't stand up, all the others, due to their arrangement, not only constitute nothing of any validity but disperse. It is in that respect that the Borromean knot is the best metaphor of the fact that we proceed only on the basis of the One.

The One engenders science. Not in the sense of the one of measurement. It is not what is measured in science that is important, contrary to what people think. What distinguishes modern science from the science of antiquity, which is based on the reciprocity between the νοῦς and the world, between what thinks and what is thought of, is precisely the function of the One, the One insofar as it is only there, we can assume, to represent solitude – the fact that the One doesn't truly knot itself with anything that resembles the sexual Other.[23] Unlike the chain, the Ones of which are all made in the same way, being nothing other than One *(de n'être rien d'autre que de l'Un).*[24]

When I said, "There's such a thing as One" *(Y a d' l'Un),* when I stressed

---

[20] See *Écrits* 539–540 and Daniel Paul Schreber's *Memoirs of My Nervous Illness* (Cambridge: Harvard University Press, 1988), 172.

[21] See *Écrits* 807. *Messages de code* could also be translated as "messages made of (or based on) code."

[22] That is, takes away their unity or oneness.

[23] There seems to be a mistake here in the French text, which reads, *qui semble à l'Autre sexuel,* literally "that seems to the sexual Other" or "that seems sexual to the Other." I have assumed, on the basis of Lacan's argument here, that the French should read *ressemble* instead of *semble.*

[24] Or "being based on nothing but One."

that, when I truly pounded that into you like an elephant all of last year, you see what I was introducing you to.

How then can we situate the function of the Other? How – if, up to a certain point, what remains of any language when it is written is based simply on knots of the One – are we to posit a difference? For it is clear that the Other cannot be added to the One. The Other can only be differentiated from it. If there is something by which it participates in the One, it is not by being added. For the Other – as I already said, but it is not clear that you heard me – is the One-missing *(l'un-en-moins)*.[25]

That's why, in any relationship of man with a woman – she who is in question *(en cause)* – it is from the perspective of the One-missing *(l'Une-en-moins)* that she must be taken up. I already indicated that to you concerning Don Juan, but, of course, there was only one person who noticed – my daughter.

4

It is not enough to have found a general solution to the problem of Borromean knots, for an infinite number of Borromean knots. We must find a way to demonstrate that it is the only solution.

But, as of our point in time today, there is no theory of knots. Currently, there is no mathematical formalization applicable to knots, apart from a few little constructions like those I showed you, that allows us to foresee that a solution like the one I just gave is not simply ex-sistent, but necessary, in other words, that it doesn't stop – as I define the necessary – being written. I'm going to show it to you right away. It suffices for me to do this.

117

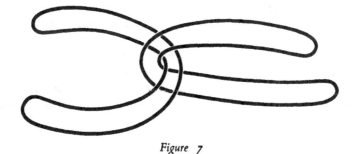

Figure 7

I just passed one of these rings around the other in such a way that they form, not the kind of bending I showed you earlier but simply a sailor's knot. You immediately see that I can, without any difficulty, pursue the

[25] This could also be translated as the "One-less" or "One-too-few."

operation on either side by making as many sailor's knots as I like, with all the rings of string in the world.

Here too I can close the chain, thereby eliminating the separability these elements had hitherto retained. I use a third ring to join the two ends of the chain.

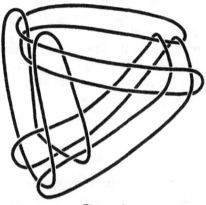

Figure 8

Here, without any doubt, we have a solution which is just as valid as the first. The knot enjoys the Borromean property that if I cut any one of the rings that I have arranged in this way, all the others are set free.

118 None of the rings here is any different from the others. There is no privileged point and the chain is strictly homogeneous. You realize that there is no topological analogy between the two ways of knotting the rings of string I showed you. In the case of the sailor's knots, there is what might be called a topology of twisting compared to the preceding one, which is simply one of bending. But it wouldn't be contradictory to use bent rings in a sailor's knot.

Hence you see that the question arises of knowing how to set a limit to the solutions of the Borromean problem. I will leave the question open.

What is at stake for us, as you have realized, is to obtain a model of mathematical formalization. Formalization is nothing other than the substitution of what is called a letter for any number of ones. What does it mean when we write that inertia is

$$\frac{mv^2}{2}$$

if not that, whatever the number of ones you place under each of those letters, you are subject to a certain number of laws – laws of grouping, addition, multiplication, etc.

Those are the questions that I am opening up, that are designed to announce to you what I hope to transmit to you concerning that which is written.

That which is written – what would that be in the end? The conditions of jouissance. And that which is counted – what would that be? The residues of jouissance. Isn't it by joining that a-sexual up with what she has by way of surplus jouissance – being, as she is, the Other, since she can only be said to be Other – that woman offers it to man in the guise of object *a?*

Man believes he creates – he believes believes believes, he creates creates creates. He creates creates creates woman. In reality, he puts her to work – to the work of the One. And it is in that respect that the Other – the Other insofar as the articulation of language, that is, the truth, is inscribed therein – the Other must be barred, barred on the basis of *(de)* what I earlier qualified as the One-missing.[26] That is what S($\cancel{A}$) means. It is in that respect that we arrive at the point of raising the question how to make the One into something that holds up, that is, that is counted without being.

Mathematization alone reaches a real – and it is in that respect that it is compatible with our discourse, analytic discourse – a real that has nothing to do with what traditional knowledge has served as a basis for, which is not what the latter believes it to be – namely, reality – but rather fantasy.

The real, I will say, is the mystery of the speaking body, the mystery of the unconscious.

May 15, 1973

Answers   119

I have transcribed here the answers Jacques Lacan gave to certain questions I asked him while I was establishing the text of this lecture. (J.A.M.)

It is remarkable that a figure as simple as that of the Borromean knot has not served as a point of departure for – a topology.

Indeed, there are several ways to approach space.

Being captivated by the notion of dimensions, that is, by cuts, is the characterology of a saw technique.[27] It is even reflected in the notion of the point, for the fact that it qualifies as one that which has, as is clearly stated, zero dimensions – that is, that which doesn't exist – says it all.

On the basis, on the contrary, of rings of string, a wedging *(coinçage)*

---

[26] The French here, perhaps erroneously, fails to capitalize the *u* of *l'un-en-moins.*
[27] See the beginning of section 2 of this chapter, where Lacan talks about a point cutting a line, a line cutting a plane, and a plane cutting a space.

occurs, since it is the crossing of two continuities that stops a third continuity. Doesn't it seem that this wedging could constitute the initial phenomenon of a topology?

It is a phenomenon that has going for it the fact of being in no point localizable. Consider but the Borromean knot – it is immediately clear that one can number three "spots" *(endroits)*, put that word in quotes, where the rings that create the knot can become wedged together.

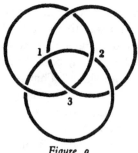

Figure 9

That assumes in each case that the two other spots get reduced to that one. Does that mean that there *is only* one? Certainly not. Though the expression "threefold point" is used, it cannot in any way satisfy the notion of a point. This point is not constituted here by the convergence of three lines, if nothing else because there are two different points – a right and a left.

For my part, I am surprised that it seems to be widely accepted that we cannot, by a message said to be informative, convey to the subject supposed by language the notion of right and left. People certainly realize that we can communicate the distinction between them, but then how are we to specify them? As opposed to a certain argument, it seems quite possible to me, precisely by dictating a flattening out that is quite conceivable on the basis of the experience of knots, if a knot is, as I believe it is, a logical fact.

Note that the flattened out (knot) is something other than a surface.

It presupposes an entirely different dit-mension than the continuity implicit in space. And that is why I use a written form of the word that designates therein the "mension" of what is said *(dit)*. That is permitted only by the llanguage that I speak – but it is not such that I need deprive myself of it inasmuch as I speak. Quite the contrary, given what I think about it – I dare say.

In other words, what is important is not that there are three dimensions in space. What is important is the Borromean knot and that for the sake of which we accede to the real it represents to us.

The illusion that we could not transmit anything to transplanetary beings regarding the specificity of right and left always seemed felicitous to me, insofar as it founds the distinction between the imaginary and the symbolic.

But right and left have nothing to do with what we learn *(appréhendons)* of them aesthetically, which means – in the relation founded by our bodies – of its *two* apparent sides.

What the Borromean knot *demonstrates* is not the fact that it is made of a ring of string, around which it suffices to bend another ring like two ears such that a third, linking the two loops, cannot become unbuckled due to the first ring. It is the fact that, of these three rings, any one of them can function as first and last, the third functioning thus as the intermediate link, that is, as the bent ears – see figures 4 and 5.

On the basis of that, the fact can be deduced that whatever the number of intermediate links – that is, of double ears – any of them can function as first and last, the others coupling them with their infinity of ears.

Those ears are thus laid out or constructed, not on the basis of a 1–2, 2–1 juxtaposition, but, in the interval between those two, on the basis of a 2–2 juxtaposition repeated as many times as there are rings minus three, namely, the number of rings in the Borromean knot.

Nevertheless, it is clear that, as the privileged links between the first ring and the second and the second to last and the last continue to be valid, the introduction of the first and the last in the central link leads to singular entanglements.

Dispensing with these, one can nevertheless refind the initial arrangement.

In their complexity, knots are well designed to make us relativize the supposed three dimensions of space, founded solely on the translation we give for our body in a solid volume.   121

Not that it doesn't lend itself anatomically to that translation. But we have here the whole question of the necessary revision – namely, of that for the sake of which it takes on that form – apparently, that is, for the sake of our gaze.

I indicate here where the mathematics of wedging, in other words, knots, could come in.

Let us take a cube and break it down into eight (2^3) little cubes, regularly stacked, the side of each little cube being half the size of that of the first cube.

Let us remove two little cubes whose vertices are at two of the diametrically opposed vertices of the large cube.

There are then two ways, and only two ways, to join the six little cubes [two by two] along their common sides.

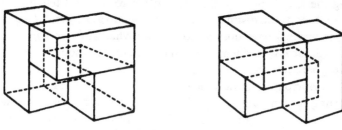

Figures 10 and 11

These two ways define two different arrangements by which to couple three full axes, according, let's say, to the directions of space distinguished by Cartesian coordinates.

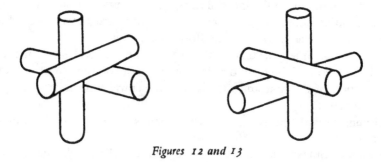

Figures 12 and 13

For each of the three axes, the two empty cubes that were removed at first allow us to define in a univocal way the inflection we can impose upon them.

122   That is the inflection required by the wedging in the Borromean knot.

But there is more. We can require the jettisoning of the privilege constituted by the existence of the first and last circle – any of them being able to play that role – in the Borromean knot, namely, that the first and the last in the said knot be constituted by providing them with a bend *(reploiement)* with the same structure as the central link – in other words, that the 2–2 link be univocal there. That is figure 8.

That which inextricably results therefrom for any attempt at flattening out *(mise-à-plat)* felicitously contrasts with the elegance of the flatness *(à-*

plat) of the original presentation (figure 3). And nevertheless, you will notice that nothing is easier than to once again isolate therein two rings, in the same positions said to be first and last in the original knot. This time, any of them can fill those roles absolutely, since the privilege has disappeared that, as I said, so seriously complicated the arrangement of the intermediary links when we were dealing with the original Borromean knot, but raised to a number greater than four.

Indeed, the links in this case are no longer constituted by the simple bending of a ring, such as we imagine it having two ears, but by bending it such that four strands of the connected link are taken up by the rings I designated with the terms "first" and "last," but not in an equivalent fashion, one of the two taking them up simply, the other – which, by dint of this very fact, is definable as different – hugging the four strands in a double loop.

Everywhere in a central link the four strands allow for a certain number of typical crossings that are subject to variation.

In short, these links are four times shorter than the extreme rings.

I conclude from this that space is not intuitive. It is a mathematician – which is what everyone can read in the history of mathematics itself.

That means that space knows how to count, not much higher than we do – and for good reason – since it is only up to six, not even seven. That is why Jahve distinguished himself with his iron-clad rule of the week.

Of course, the man in the street goes up to ten, but that's because he counts on his fingers. He has had to back off, since with the zero, that is, he is wrong – one mustn't count on anything that is an apparent body or an animal movement. What is amusing is that science did not at first detach itself except at the cost of a 6 x 10, that is, a sexagisimal system – see the Babylonians.

To return to space, it seems to be part and parcel of the unconscious – structured like a language.

And if it counts up to six, it is because it can only refind the two via the three of revelation.

One more word – one must invent nothing. That is what the revelation of the unconscious teaches us. But there is nothing to be done – invention itches until we scratch. Because what is necessary is to turn away from the real and from what the presence of number signifies.   123

One word to finish. You might have noticed that collapsing *(homogénéisation)* the *extreme* links into one is not the same thing as hooking them together end to end, which, strangely enough, had no more effect on the chain than to leave them independent, except for the number of links, which it reduces by one.

What result can we expect from the original chain with three links when we operate thereupon as well? Its reduction to two links that would assuredly come apart if either of them is cut.

But how will they be wound?

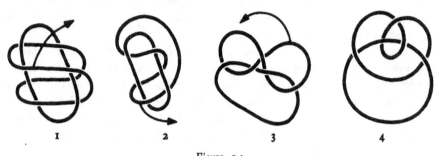

Figure *14*

There will be a simple ring with an inner eight wound around it,[28] the same inner eight with which I symbolize the subject – allowing us hence to recognize in the simple ring, which, moreover, can be transposed into *(s'intervertit avec)* the eight, the sign of object *a* – namely, the cause by which the subject identifies with his desire.

October 22, 1973

[28] What I have translated here as the "inner eight" is rendered in Alan Sheridan's 1978 translation of Seminar XI, *The Four Fundamental Concepts of Psychoanalysis,* as the "interior eight."

XI

The rat in the maze

LANGUAGE IS KNOWLEDGE'S HAREBRAINED LUCUBRATION
ABOUT LLANGUAGE.
THE UNITY OF THE BODY.
THE LACANIAN HYPOTHESIS.
LOVE, FROM CONTINGENCY TO NECESSITY.

Thanks to someone who is willing to polish up what I tell you here, four or five days ago I received the nicely scrubbed truffle in my elocutions this year.

With this title, *Encore,* I wasn't sure, I must admit, that I was still in the field I have cleared for twenty years, since what it said was that it could still *(encore)* go on a long time. Rereading the first transcription of this Seminar, I found that it wasn't so bad, especially given that I began with a formulation that seemed a tad trivial to me, that the Other's jouissance is not the sign of love. It was a point of departure I could perhaps come back to today in closing what I opened at that time.

I spoke a bit of love. Yet the crux of or key to what I put forward this year concerns the status of knowledge, and I stressed that the use *(exercice)*[1] of knowledge could but imply *(représenter)* a jouissance. That is what I'd like to add to today by a reflection concerning what is done in a groping manner in scientific discourse with respect to what can be produced by way of knowledge.

1

To get right to the point – knowledge is an enigma.

That enigma is presented to us by the unconscious, as it is revealed by analytic discourse. That enigma is enunciated as follows: for the speaking being, knowledge is that which is articulated. People could have noticed that a long time ago, because in tracing out the pathways of knowledge they were doing nothing but articulate things, centering them for a long time on being. Now it is obvious that nothing is, if not insofar as it is said that it is.

---

[1] *Exercice* could also be translated as "implementation," "putting into use," "putting into effect," "exercising," or "exercise."

I call that S₂. You have to know how to hear that – is it of them-two *(est-ce bien d'eux)*[2] that it speaks? It is generally said that language serves to communicate. To communicate about what, one must ask oneself, about which them *(eux)?* Communication implies reference. But one thing is clear – language is merely what scientific discourse elaborates to account for what I call llanguage.

Llanguage serves purposes that are altogether different from that of communication. That is what the experience of the unconscious has shown us, insofar as it is made of llanguage, which, as you know, I write with two l's to designate what each of us deals with, our so-called mother tongue *(lalangue dite maternelle)*, which isn't called that by accident.

If communication approaches what is effectively at work in the jouissance of llanguage, it is because communication implies a reply, in other words, dialogue. But does llanguage serve, first and foremost, to dialogue? As I have said before, nothing is less certain.

I just got hold of an important book by an author named Bateson about which people had talked my ears off, enough to get on my nerves a bit. I should say that it was given to me by someone who had been touched by the grace of a certain text of mine he translated into his language, adding some commentary to it,[3] and who felt he had found in Bateson's work something that went significantly further than "the unconscious structured like a language."

Now Bateson, not realizing that the unconscious is structured like a language, has but a rather mediocre conception of it. But he creates some very nice artifices he calls "metalogues." They're not bad, insofar as they involve, if we take him at his word, some internal, dialectical progress, being produced only by examining the evolution of a term's meaning. As has always been the case in everything that has been called a dialogue, the point is to make the supposed interlocutor say what motivates the speaker's very question, in other words, to incarnate in the other the answer that is already there. It's in that sense that dialogues, classical dialogues – the finest examples of which are represented by the Platonic legacy – are shown not to be dialogues.

If I have said that language is what the unconscious is structured like, that is because language, first of all, doesn't exist. Language is what we try to know concerning the function of llanguage.

---

[2] Lacan is playing off of the homophony between *d'eux*, of them, and *deux*, two, and between *S* and *est-ce*.

[3] Anthony Wilden translated Lacan's "Function and Field of Speech and Language in Psychoanalysis" in *The Language of the Self* (Baltimore: Johns Hopkins, 1968); he talked to Lacan about Gregory Bateson's book, *Steps to an Ecology of Mind* (New York: Ballantine, 1972). The whole discussion of "learning" (above all, of rat research based on "trial and error") in this chapter of the Seminar seems to be a response to Bateson's work.

Certainly, it is thus that scientific discourse itself approaches language, except that it is difficult for scientific discourse to fully actualize language, since it misrecognizes the unconscious. The unconscious evinces knowledge that, for the most part, escapes the speaking being. That being provides the occasion to realize just how far the effects of llanguage go, in that   127
it presents all sorts of affects that remain enigmatic. Those affects are what result from the presence of llanguage insofar as it articulates things by way of knowledge *(de savoir)*[4] that go much further than what the speaking being sustains *(supporte)* by way of enunciated knowledge.

Language is, no doubt, made up of llanguage. It is knowledge's harebrained lucubration *(élucubration)* about llanguage. But the unconscious is knowledge, a knowing how to do things *(savoir-faire)* with llanguage. And what we know how to do with llanguage goes well beyond what we can account for under the heading of language.

Llanguage affects us first of all by everything it brings with it by way of effects that are affects. If we can say that the unconscious is structured like a language, it is in the sense that the effects of llanguage, already there qua knowledge, go well beyond anything the being who speaks is capable of enunciating.

It is in that regard that the unconscious, insofar as I base it on its deciphering, can only be structured like a language, a language that is always hypothetical with respect to what supports it, namely, llanguage. Llanguage is what allowed me to turn my S_2 into a question earlier and ask – is it truly a question *of them-two (d'eux)* in language?

Stated otherwise, it has become clear, thanks to analytic discourse, that language is not simply communication. Misrecognizing that fact, a grimace has emerged in the lowest depths of science that consists in asking how being can know anything whatsoever. My question today regarding knowledge will hinge on that.

2

How can being know? It's amusing to see how this question is supposedly answered. Since the limit, as I have posited it, is constituted by the fact that there are beings who speak, people wonder what the knowledge of those who do not speak could be. They wonder about it. They don't know why they wonder about it. But they wonder about it all the same. So they build a little maze *(labyrinthe)* for rats.

They hope thereby to be on the right track by which to determine what knowledge is. They believe a rat is going to show the capacity it has to learn

---

[4] The French, *de savoir*, could also be translated as "by knowing," "since it knows," "qua knowledge," or "regarding knowledge."

(apprendre). To learn *(A-prendre)*[5] to do what? What interests it, of course. And what do they assume interests it?

They do not take the rat as a being, but rather as a body, which means that they view it as a unit, a rat-unit. Now what thus sustains the rat's being? They don't wonder about that at all. Or rather, they identify its being with its body.

People have always imagined that being had to contain a sort of fullness that is characteristic of it. Being is a body. That is where people began in first approaching being, and they laboriously concocted *(élucubré)* a whole hierarchy of beings. Ultimately, they began with the notion that each one should know what keeps it in being *(maintenait à l'être)*[6] – that had to be its good, in other words, what gives it pleasure.

What change thus came about in discourse in order for people to suddenly question that being regarding the means it might have to go beyond itself, that is, to learn more than it needs to know in its being to survive as a body?

The maze leads not only to nourishment but to a button or flap that the supposed subject of this being must figure out how to use to obtain nourishment. Or it has to recognize a feature, a lit or colored feature, to which the being is capable of reacting. What is important is that the question of knowledge is transformed here into that of learning. If, after a series of trials and errors – "trials and errors" was left in English (in the translation) considering the people who carved out this approach to knowledge – the rate diminishes sufficiently, they note that the rat-unit is capable of learning something.

The question that is only secondarily raised – the one that interests me – is whether the rat-unit can learn how to learn. Therein lies the true mainspring of the experiment. Once it has taken one of these tests, will a rat, faced with another test of the same kind, learn more quickly? That can be easily attested to by a decrease in the number of trials necessary for it to know how it must behave in such a montage – let us call the maze, taken in conjunction with the flaps and buttons that function here, a "montage."

The question has been so rarely raised, though it has been raised, that people haven't even dreamt of investigating the differential effect of having

[5] By breaking *apprendre* ("to learn") down into *a-prendre,* Lacan seems to be pointing to the taking or grasping in learning, the taking by the rat of what interests it.

[6] Lacan's French here is quite idiosyncratic, since *maintenir* is a transitive verb. Lacan seems to construct his phraseology here along the lines of the expression *se tenir à quelque chose* (to hold onto or cleave to something); a more idiomatic translation would be "everyone should know what keeps him going (or alive)." Alternatively, the phrase could be understood as "everyone should know what keeps him alive as a body," for *l'être* could be taken as "to be it," *it* referring to the body.

the themes one proposes to the rat – by which it demonstrates its ability to learn – come from the same source or from two different sources, and of having the experimenter who teaches the rat to learn be the same or different. Now, the experimenter is the one who knows something in this business, and it is with what he knows that he invents this montage consisting of the maze, buttons, and flaps. If he were not someone whose relation to knowledge is grounded in a relation to llanguage, in the inhabiting of llanguage or the cohabitation with llanguage, there would be no montage.

The only thing the rat-unit learns in this case is to give a sign, a sign of its presence as unit. The flap is recognized only by a sign and pressing its paw on this sign is a sign. It is always by making a sign that the unit accedes to that on the basis of which one concludes that there is learning. But this relation to signs is external. Nothing confirms that the rat grasps the mechanism to which pressing the button leads. That's why the only thing that counts is to know if the experimenter notes that the rat has not only figured it out, but learned *(appris)* how a mechanism is to be grasped *(se prend)*, in other words, learned what must be grasped *(à-prendre)*. If we take the status of unconscious knowledge into account, we must examine the maze experiment in terms of how the rat-unit responds to what has been thought up by the experimenter not on the basis of nothing, but on the basis of llanguage. | 129

One doesn't invent just any old labyrinthine composition, and whether it comes from the same experimenter or two different experimenters is worth investigating. But nothing that I have been able to gather to date from this literature indicates that any such question has been raised.

This example thus leaves the questions regarding the status of knowledge and the status of learning *(apprentissage)* completely intact and distinct. The status of knowledge raises another question, namely, how it is taught.

3

It is on the basis of the notion of a kind of knowledge that is transmitted, integrally transmitted, that a sifting occurred in knowledge, thanks to which the discourse called scientific discourse was constituted.

It wasn't constituted without numerous misadventures. *Hypotheses non fingo*, Newton believed he could say, "I assume nothing." But it was on the basis of a hypothesis that the famous revolution – which wasn't at all Copernican, but rather Newtonian – hinged, substituting "it falls" for "it turns." The Newtonian hypothesis consisted in positing that the astral turning is the same as falling. But in order to observe that – which allows one to eliminate the hypothesis – he first had to make the hypothesis.

To introduce a scientific discourse concerning knowledge, one must

investigate knowledge where it is. That knowledge, insofar as it resides in
the shelter of llanguage, means the unconscious. I do not enter there, no
more than did Newton, without a hypothesis.

My hypothesis is that the individual who is affected by the unconscious
is the same individual who constitutes what I call the subject of a signifier.
That is what I enunciate in the minimal formulation that a signifier represents a subject to another signifier. The signifier in itself is nothing but what
can be defined as a difference from another signifier. It is the introduction
of difference as such into the field, which allows one to extract from llanguage the nature of the signifier *(ce qu'il en est du signifiant)*.

Stated otherwise, I reduce the hypothesis, according to the very formulation that lends it substance, to the following: it is necessary to the functioning of llanguage. To say that there is a subject is nothing other than to say
that there is a hypothesis. The only proof we have that the subject coincides
with this hypothesis, and that it is the speaking individual on whom it is
based, is that the signifier becomes a sign.

It is because there is the unconscious – namely, llanguage, insofar as it is
on the basis of the cohabitation with llanguage that a being known as speaking being is defined – that the signifier can be called upon to constitute a
sign *(faire signe)*.[7] You can take "sign" here as you like, even as the English
"thing."

The signifier is a subject's sign. Qua formal medium *(support)*, the signifier hits something other *(atteint un autre)* than what it is quite crudely as
signifier, an other that it affects and that is made into a subject of the signifier, or at least which passes for such *(pour l'être)*. It is in that respect that
the subject turns out to be – and this is only true for speaking beings – a
being *(un étant)* whose being is always elsewhere, as the predicate shows.[8]
The subject is never more than fleeting *(ponctuel)* and vanishing, for it is a
subject only by a signifier and to another signifier.

It is here that we must return to Aristotle. In a choice guided by we know
not what, Aristotle decided not to give any other definition of the individual
than the body – the body as organism, as what maintains itself as one, and
not as what reproduces. We are still hovering around the difference between
the Platonic idea and the Aristotelian definition of the individual as grounding being. The question that arises for the biologist is to know how a body
reproduces. What is in question in any work in so-called molecular chemis-
try is to know how something can be precipitated thanks to the combination

130

---

[7] *Faire signe*, like *faire l'homme*, has several meanings: "to play the part of a
sign"; "to make, create, or constitute a sign"; and to "signal or give a sign (of life,
for example)."
[8] The predicate here is presumably "speaking" in the expression "speaking
being."

of a certain number of things in a special soup[9] – for example, the fact that a bacterium begins to reproduce.

What then is the body? Is it or isn't it knowledge of the one?

Knowledge of the one turns out *(se révèle)* not to come from the body. The little we can say about knowledge of the one comes from the signifier "One." Does the signifier "One" derive from the fact that a signifier as such is never anything but *one-among-others*, referred to those others, being but its difference from the others? The question has been so little resolved to date that I devoted my whole seminar last year to accentuating this "There's such a thing as One" *(Y a d' l'Un)*.

What does "There's such a thing as One" mean? From the *one-among-others* – and the point is to know whether it is any old which one – arises an S_1, a signifying swarm,[10] a buzzing swarm. If I raise the question, "Is it of them-two that I am speaking?", I will write this S_1 of each signifier, first on the basis of its relation to S_2.[11] And you can add as many of them as you like. This is the swarm I am talking about.

$$S_1(S_1(S_1(S_1 \rightarrow S_2)))$$

S_1, the swarm or master signifier, is that which assures the unity, the unity of the subject's copulation with knowledge. It is in llanguage and nowhere else, insofar as llanguage is investigated qua language, that what a primitive linguistics designated with the term $\sigma\tau o\iota\chi\epsilon\hat{\iota} o\nu$,[12] element – and that was no accident – can be discerned. The signifier "One" is not just any old signifier. It is the signifying order insofar as it is instituted on the basis of the envelopment by which the whole of the chain subsists.

131

I recently read the work of a person who investigates the relation of S_1 to S_2, which that person takes to be a relation of representation. S_1 is supposed [by that person] to be related to S_2 insofar as it represents a subject. Whether that relation is symmetrical, antisymmetrical, transitive, or other, whether the subject is transferred from S_2 to an S_3 and so on and so forth, these questions must be taken up on the basis of the schema that I am once again providing here.

The One incarnated in llanguage is something that remains indeterminate *(indécis)* between the phoneme, the word, the sentence, and even the whole of thought. That is what is at stake in what I call the master signifier. It is the signifier One, and it was no accident that, in order to illustrate the

---

[9] Likely to be referred to now as the primal ooze or soup, instead of as a "unique bath" *(bain unique)*.

[10] *Essaim*, which I have translated here as "swarm," is pronounced in French exactly like S_1.

[11] Recall that S_2 and *est-ce d'eux* are homonyms in French.

[12] This Greek term means "constituent," "element," "first principle," "primary matter," "letter of the alphabet," or "element of knowledge."

One, I brought to our last meeting[13] that bit of string, insofar as it constitutes a ring, whose possible knot with another ring I began to investigate.

I won't pursue that point any further today, since we have been deprived of a class due to exams at this university.

4

To change the subject, I will say that what is important in what has been revealed by psychoanalytic discourse – and one is surprised not to see its thread everywhere – is that knowledge, which structures the being who speaks on the basis of a specific cohabitation, is closely related to love. All love is based on a certain relationship between two unconscious knowledges.

If I have enunciated that the subject supposed to know is what motivates transference, that is but a particular, specific application of what we find in our experience. I'll ask you to look at the text of what I enunciated here, in the middle of this year, regarding the choice of love. I spoke, ultimately, of recognition, recognition – via signs that are always punctuated enigmatically – of the way in which being is affected qua subject of unconscious knowledge.

There's no such thing as a sexual relationship because one's jouissance of the Other taken as a body is always inadequate – perverse, on the one hand, insofar as the Other is reduced to object a, and crazy and enigmatic, on the other, I would say. Isn't it on the basis of the confrontation with this impasse, with this impossibility by which a real is defined, that love is put to the test? Regarding one's partner, love can only actualize what, in a sort of poetic flight, in order to make myself understood, I called courage – courage with respect to this fatal destiny. But is it courage that is at stake or pathways of recognition? That recognition is nothing other than the way in which the relationship said to be sexual – that has now become a subject-to-subject relationship, the subject being but the effect of unconscious knowledge – stops not being written.

"To stop not being written" is not a formulation proffered haphazardly. I associated it with contingency, whereas I delighted in [characterizing] the necessary as that which "doesn't stop being written," for the necessary is not the real. Let us note in passing that the displacement of this negation raises for us the question of the nature of negation when it takes the place of a non-existence. I have also defined the sexual relationship as that which "doesn't stop not being written." There is an impossibility therein. It is also that nothing can speak it – there is no existence of the sexual relationship

132

13 The French here erroneously reads "second to last meeting."

in the act of speaking. But what does it mean to negate it *(nier)?* Is it in any way legitimate to substitute a negation for the proven apprehension of the non-existence? That too is a question I shall merely raise here. Does the word "interdiction" mean any more, is it any more permitted? That cannot be immediately determined either.

I incarnated contingency in the expression "stops not being written." For here there is nothing but encounter, the encounter in the partner of symptoms and affects, of everything that marks in each of us the trace of his exile – not as subject but as speaking – his exile from the sexual relationship. Isn't that tantamount to saying that it is owing only to the affect that results from this gap that something is encountered, which can vary infinitely as to level of knowledge, but which momentarily gives the illusion that the sexual relationship stops not being written? – an illusion that something is not only articulated but inscribed, inscribed in each of our destinies, by which, for a while – a time during which things are suspended – what would constitute the sexual relationship finds its trace and its mirage-like path in the being who speaks. The displacement of the negation from the "stops not being written" to the "doesn't stop being written," in other words, from contingency to necessity – there lies the point of suspension to which all love is attached.

All love, subsisting only on the basis of the "stops not being written," tends to make the negation shift to the "doesn't stop being written," doesn't stop, won't stop.

Such is the substitute that – by the path of existence, not of the sexual relationship, but of the unconscious, which differs therefrom – constitutes the destiny as well as the drama of love.

Given the time, which is that at which I normally desire to take leave of you, I won't take things any further here – I will simply indicate that what I have said of hatred is not related to the level at which the hold *(prise)* of unconscious knowledge is articulated.

The subject can't not desire not to know too much about the nature of the eminently contingent encounter with the other. Thus he shifts [his focus] from the other to the being that is caught up therein.

The relation of being to being is not the relation of harmony that was   133
prepared for us throughout the ages, though we don't really know why, by a whole tradition in which Aristotle, who saw therein only supreme jouissance, converges with Christianity, for which it is beatitude. That gets us bogged down in a mirage-like apprehension. For it is love that approaches being as such in the encounter.

Isn't it in love's approach to being that something emerges that makes being into what is only sustained by the fact of missing each other *(se rater)?*[14] I spoke of rats earlier – that was what was at stake. It's no accident people chose rats. It's because one can easily make a unit of it – the rat can be "eraticated."[15] I already saw that at a time when I had a concierge, when I lived in the rue de la Pompe – the concierge never missed *(ratait)* a rat. His hatred for rats was equal to the rat's being.

Doesn't the extreme of love, true love, reside in the approach to being? And true love – analytic experience assuredly didn't make this discovery, borne witness to by the eternal modulation of themes on love – true love gives way to hatred.

There – I'm leaving you.

Shall I say, "See you next year"? You'll notice that I've never ever said that to you. For a very simple reason – which is that I've never known, for the last twenty years, if I would continue the next year. That is part and parcel of my destiny as object *a.*

After ten years, my podium *(parole)* was taken away from me. It turns out, for reasons wherein destiny played a part, as did my inclination to please certain people, that I continued for ten more *(encore)* years. I have thus closed the twenty-year cycle. Will I continue next year? Why not stop the *encore* now?

What is truly admirable is that no one ever doubted that I would continue. The fact that I am making this remark nevertheless raises the question. It could, after all, happen that to the *encore* I add – "That's enough."

Well, I'll leave it for you to place bets on. There are many who believe they know me and who think that I find herein an infinite satisfaction. Next to the amount of work it involves, I must say that that seems pretty minimal to me. So place your bets.

And what will the result be? Will it mean that those who have guessed correctly love me? Well – that is precisely the meaning of what I just enunciated for you today – to know what your partner will do is not a proof of love.

June 26, 1973

[14] "Missing" should be understood here in the sense of missing the mark, not missing someone who is far away.
[15] The French here, *ça se rature,* literally means "can be erased, struck out, crossed out," etc.

INDEX